Y0-BOE-830

FOUNDATIONS AND NEW FRONTIERS IN DIVERSITY, EQUITY, AND INCLUSION

LeRoy Thompson, Ph.D.

Archway Publishing books may be ordered through booksellers or by contacting:

Archway Publishing
1663 Liberty Drive
Bloomington, IN 47403
www.archwaypublishing.com
844-669-3957

ISBN: 978-1-6657-5451-4 (sc)
ISBN: 978-1-6657-5452-1 (e)

Library of Congress Control Number: 2023923887

Print information available on the last page.

Archway Publishing rev. date: 01/27/2024

CONTENTS

Prologue vii

Section 1: Foundations

Chapter 1   Diversity, Equity, and Inclusion: A History 1
Chapter 2   The Neurobiology of Bias 10
Chapter 3   Diversity and Cultural Awareness 19

Section 2: New Frontiers

Chapter 4   The Quest for Equity 33
Chapter 5   The Power of Inclusion 50
Chapter 6   Keys to Successful DEI Initiatives 65
Chapter 7   DEI and Change Management 77

Epilogue 89

PROLOGUE

The United States workforce is more diverse than ever before. The world has become a global marketplace, and smart companies must leverage diversity to compete. There is hard evidence that organizations that embrace diversity, equity, and inclusion (we'll use the acronym DEI throughout) in the right ways consistently outperform their competitors. Indeed, companies whose corporate leadership is more diverse in terms of ethnicity, gender, and other cultural backgrounds have higher productivity than their counterparts with lower levels of diversity.

This is not a new concept, but it has taken years of research to prove that it does have an impact on individual, team, and business outcomes. One of the goals of this book is to explore the "business case" for diversity. To this effect, I hope that this book provides the next generation of DEI decision-makers with the appropriate knowledge and skills they need to create equitable and inclusive organizations now and in the future.

This book also seeks to guide the daily actions of decision-makers who want to help their organizations do well. To this end, this book will help you develop a sustainable organizational strategy when it comes to working with DEI.

This book is arranged into seven chapters that address both the principles and the practices of doing DEI work in organizations. The remaining portion of this introduction will provide an overview about what you can hope to expect in the upcoming chapters in terms of content and new understandings.

Chapter 1 addresses historical foundations of diversity work, documenting the major shifts and transitions in the field. Throughout the decades, diversity work has taken on new meaning. At its core, the work has been centered around creating practices that include people of all backgrounds and creating organizational cultures that value diverse perspectives. Knowledge of the history and—more importantly—the current sociopolitical landscape around the work, allows for greater opportunities when it comes to working with differences. It will hopefully also help you avoid many of the mistakes and missteps of past DEI efforts.

Chapter 2 explores the neurobiology of bias—a key component of diversity, equity, and inclusion initiatives. Our brain impacts a wide variety of outcomes in terms of our actions, behaviors, cognitions, and perceptions. Through an exploration of psychological threat and safety, this chapter addresses how bias is formed and—more importantly— how to disrupt bias from the "bottom up". If we understand that bias is a series of cognitive processes, we can work toward responding versus reacting when encountering the new and different.

Chapter 3 addresses the various dimensions of human differences and how they impact everyday outcomes and behaviors in the workplace. This chapter will explore how diversity and the related concepts of equity and inclusion impact individual, team, and organizational performance. This chapter will also explore how diversity impacts recruitment and retention, upward mobility, promotion rates, compensation, etc.

Chapter 4 will examine the quest for equity, looking specifically at the root causes of systemic bias. This chapter will take a deep dive into racial equity in the workplace and explore the ways in which racial membership has impacted the pursuit of fairness in organizational practices and procedures. In this chapter, race is used as the system of analysis, but the process can be applied to nearly every aspect of difference (e.g., ability, age, gender, sexual orientation, and even religion).

Chapter 5 explores the power of inclusion. This chapter will examine psychological, and sometimes physical, barriers to individuals' and groups' full participation in the workplace. This chapter will also explore the impact of in-groups and out-groups in organizational settings. The chapter seeks to address the ways in which decision-makers can create psychologically safe and welcoming cultures.

Chapter 6 takes into account what we know about diversity, equity, and inclusion work so far. This chapter provides helpful guidance when it comes to doing action-oriented research in your own organization, analyzing key data and metrics as they relate to diversity, equity, and inclusion issues as well as methods to engage other organizational members in fostering equity and inclusion.

Finally, chapter 7 details new frontiers when it comes to diversity work and change. As with any change effort, expect resistance; it is a natural part of the process. Through overcommunicating and using all available channels, you can help reinforce positive outcomes.

In each of these chapters, I'll offer specific tools and techniques for managing diversity along with examples that demonstrate the ideas and methods in action. To this effect, this book is a guide that organizational decision-makers can use to deal with diversity dynamics that are at the root of many organizational problems.

Based on many years of consulting experience with over 180 clients in the private, public, and nonprofit sectors, *Foundations and New Frontiers in Diversity, Equity, and Inclusion* describes the current understanding of best practices, strategic priorities, and organizational rationale when it comes to working with the primary dimensions of diversity. By the end of this text, you should be well equipped to:

1. Know the difference between diversity, equity, and inclusion
2. Understand the critical social and cognitive processes related to DEI work

3. Build out the framework for implementing a DEI initiative or for a singular focus on equity
4. Help others troubleshoot problems and spot emerging opportunities when it comes to issues of diversity, equity, and inclusion initiatives

Concluding Comments

For most of my professional career, my goal has been to help clients develop a culture of equity and inclusion at all levels of their organizations. I think we have made this process much more difficult than it has to be. I hope that the book will make it easier. I also hope it will help you develop skills as it relates to implementing recruitment plans, retaining diverse pipelines, fostering workplace equity, and conquering bias, among others. Remember, no matter what role you have in your organization, you have the capacity to use diversity as a source of competitive advantage.

CHAPTER 1

DIVERSITY, EQUITY, AND INCLUSION: A HISTORY

The struggle with ethnic and gender diversity is also not new; diversity has, of course, been a fundamental part of our society since the country's inception. In the beginning, people came from all over the world—some by choice, others by force—to be a part of the American system of wealth, opportunity, and prosperity. While the influx of foreign contributors ensured that America grew quickly, it also came with its unique set of challenges—particularly when it came to ethnicity.

In recent years, there has been a greater shift in understanding regarding working with and addressing diversity, creating equitable practices, and building inclusive workforces. Diversity work for the past half century has existed in waves that can best be characterized as a series of social movements aimed at changing attitudes and behaviors.[1] Reviewing the previous waves when it comes to diversity work serves as an important orientation point for current and future work in the field.

---

[1] Maltbia, T. E., and Power, A. T. (2008). *A Leader's Guide to Leveraging Diversity: Strategic Learning Capabilities for Breakthrough Performance.* Routledge.

The Social Construct of Race

Much of the current focus in DEI has been specifically on "racial equity." The reality is that "race" as a distinguishing factor between people does not exist. In both the biological and social sciences, race is considered a social construct. When I say that race is a social construct—an idea introduced by W. E. B. Dubois over a hundred years ago—I mean that it is a subjective classification system with no foundation in genetics. Race is the combination of meanings assigned to various groups rather than a fundamental difference between groups. The term "racism" gets widely misused. Technically speaking, it is inaccurate to refer to an individual person as a "racist". Interesting, right? An individual who harbors an explicit bias again someone based on that person's race is termed "bigoted". "Racism" is specifically defined as a systemic effect.

Over time, the meaning assigned to different groups and their labels have changed. Take for example the plight of African Americans. At first, being "Black" was an analysis of how much African blood you had. However, over the decades, the requirements changed. It used to be a drop. Now being African American is much more complex. The same is true for Mexican ancestry whose "racial" classification changed in the 1900's from "Mexican" to "White" to "Non-White" and then back to "Mexican" before the concept of "Hispanic" was introduced in the 1970s.

Thus, a distinction at this point should be made between race and ethnicity. When you think of race, you are most likely thinking of the hierarchical system developed in the 16th century and further codified in the 18th century. It places some groups of people in a higher order of value and capacity than others. In America, "racial groups" have been historically stratified with European Americans at the top, African Americans at the bottom, and Asian Americans, Arabic Americans, and Latinx Americans located somewhere in between.[2] However, when we think about ethnicity, the connotation switches to a more accurate undressing of differences of customs, foods, traditions, etc. This is a far more helpful orientation. I'll continue to use the term *race* throughout as it has become a convenient, if inaccurate, norm. At this stage, there's really no way to not talk about "race". We'll also be using "racioethnic" and "racioethnicity" throughout. These terms are used to refer to the combination of sociocultural and physical differences that account for membership in specific identity groups.

The Civil Rights Era and Beyond

The first wave of diversity work really took off in the 1950s and 1960s during the civil rights era, when ethnic minorities and women began to voice their concerns about injustice embedded in many US institutions. As a result, the 1964 Civil Rights Act was passed to prohibit discrimination on the basis of race, color, religion, sex, or national origin. Places of employment were legally forbidden to exercise unjust treatment during the hiring, promotion, or firing processes. Organizations also became more cognizant of the issues of equity and fairness and hired more diverse populations as a result.

As ethnic minorities and women began to enter the workplace in record numbers, they encountered barriers in systems that were not created for them. Issues of racial and sexual discrimination became more prevalent, which resulted in affirmative action legislation and equal opportunity employment laws in the 1970s to protect new classes of workers.

By the 1980s, the concept of "diversity" really started to take hold. At this time, there was a greater emphasis on fostering cross-cultural awareness and leveraging the power of differences. This was also when

---

[2] Abdalla, S. (2018). *Experiences of Faculty Women of Color: A Literature Review.* Online submission.

organizations started to put two and two together when it came to the business case of diversity. During this phase, there was a greater reliance on understanding differences and fostering open dialogue across cultures. This era of "valuing diversity" was characterized by a greater focus on inclusivity as a strategy for economic gain and business productivity.

While more women and ethnic minorities were in the workforce than ever before, they also were under undue pressure to assimilate to the corporate culture. Indeed, the "old boys club"[3] and company cultures that perpetuated systemic bias and discrimination were still rampant. Thus, while the diversification of the workforce was high, organizational members who did not share the founders' backgrounds in terms of race, ethnicity, and/or gender often felt restricted in their actions and behaviors. Yes, organizations were more diverse than ever before, but at the cost of expression for many members.

The 1990s Revival

During the 1990s, the Federal Glass Ceiling Commission began to study the barriers that were impacting underrepresented members in the workplace. What became clear was that if organizations were to have truly equitable systems, organizational decision-makers needed to align their practices, foster inclusive cultures, and truly embrace the business case for differences.

Luminaries in the field, such as Judith Katz, Roosevelt Thomas, and Price Cobbs, set the stage for forward-thinking work on aligning organizational systems. For the first time, a variety of tools were developed to increase organizations' cultural awareness around the multiple dimensions of diversity.

One of my earliest encounters with the complexity of diversity

---

[3] "Old boys club" refers to the informal network of nepotism among White men of high socioeconomic rank.

work came during this time when I was working on a project in a large municipality. I was retained by a leadership council that was tasked with helping organizations uncover and work through their implicit biases when it came to race. The head of the council at that time, although not a person of color, was by all accounts an ally in the work. During our sessions with organizational leaders, it was suggested that it would be a good use of my time and theirs if I berated the audience and let them know just how racist they were. I couldn't believe the ask, let alone the deeper intentions. Not only was this completely out of my character, but it was counterproductive in so many ways. Putting people on the defensive, creating a sense of guilt for past inequities, and shaming them for their lack of cultural awareness was the go-to tactic at this stage. Sadly, I have seen these practices used in DEI work today. Believe me I was (and still am) deeply committed to the advancement of my people. But for one, guilt and shame rarely produce forward momentum. You don't change someone's mind by denigrating them. And two, there are much more impactful ways of showing someone how "racist" they may be. We'll talk more about this later.

Being tasked with helping others uncover their biases when it came to race and ethnicity, helped me realize two additional things. First, that unconscious bias was operating in the here and now, and second, that there is a profound need to understand the ways in which differences impact our decision-making and functioning. It was one of the first moments when I realized how deeply rooted bias could operate. In this setting—with professional diversity experts who touted egalitarian values and who believed that they were nonprejudiced—I was being subjected to the very bias we were attempting to disrupt. It also highlighted the fact that the conditions must be set to have productive dialogue when it comes to differences. No matter how angry one might be about the injustices that have been perpetuated, we must find time and space for productive dialogue. At the same time, that dialogue cannot be allowed to weaken the imperative of seeing real systemic change in how people are treated. This may have been one of my earliest encounters with implicit bias, but it was not the last.

Social Justice in the 2000s

In the 2000s, diversity, equity, and inclusion work became almost synonymous with the idea of collective impact and social justice. The last two decades have seen a rise in social activism campaigns that were focused on achieving equitable outcomes for various groups of people including the #BlackLivesMatter movement fighting against racial discrimination against Blacks/African Americans and the #MeToo movement fighting against gender discrimination against women.

At the same time, current events have put individuals like Trayvon Martin,[4] Eric Garner,[5] Ahmaud Arbery,[6] Breonna Taylor,[7] and George Floyd[8] into the headlines. The death of African Americans at the hands of the police and private citizens has strengthened the need for having conversations about differences of all types. Thus, the recent push toward creating equitable practices and organizational systems takes on new meaning, considering current sociopolitical pressures.

Over a third of US workers over the age of sixteen are ethnic

---

[4] Trayvon Martin was a seventeen-year-old boy killed on February 26, 2012, in Sanford, Florida, by George Zimmerman, the neighborhood watch coordinator of his gated community.

[5] Eric Garner was a forty-three-year-old man killed in Staten Island, New York, on July 17, 2014, in the custody of the New York Police Department.

[6] Ahmaud Arbery was a twenty-five-year-old African American man killed by Travis and Gregory McMichael in Glynn County, Georgia, on February 23, 2020.

[7] Breonna Taylor was a twenty-six-year-old African American woman killed in Louisville, Kentucky, by the Louisville Metro Police Department on March 13, 2020.

[8] George Floyd, a forty-six-year-old African American man, was killed by Derek Chauvin, a member of the Minneapolis Police Department, on May 25, 2020.

minority members.[9] The workforce is also pretty diverse when it comes to gender in the simplest sense, with nearly half of the workforce identifying as female.[10] Taken together, these statistics suggest that the workplace, by most accounts, has members from multiple backgrounds.

The problem lies in the fact that this representation does not usually translate into the upper levels of management and senior leadership. Thus, the bulk of influential decision-making occurs among individuals who are primarily White[11] and male.[12] This still poses a challenge for racioethnic minority members and women who may find it hard to ascend the corporate ladder due to real and perceived barriers that can be systemically baked into the fabric of the organization.

Nearly all major companies feel the need to maintain a visible commitment to diversity (see Table 1). Yet there is a big difference between touting the value of diversity and actually implementing DEI. In theory, diversity is highly important but taking a closer look at the outcomes for diverse members would suggest otherwise. Indeed, "Fortune 100" companies like Amazon, Pinterest, McDonald's, and Uber have been the subject of allegations of racial and gender-based discrimination in recent years, making the need for creating more equitable cultures even more apparent.

---

[9] Labor Force Statistics from the Current Population Survey, https://www.bls.gov/cps/cpsaat11.htm.

[10] Labor Force Statistics from the Current Population Survey, https://www.bls.gov/cps/cpsaat11.htm.

[11] Roberson, L., and Block, C. J. (2001). "Racioethnicity and Job Performance: A Review and Critique of Theoretical Perspectives on the Causes of Group Differences." *Research in Organizational Behavior*, 23, 247–325.

[12] Gipson, A. N., Pfaff, D. L., Mendelsohn, D. B., Catenacci, L. T., and Burke, W. W. (2017). "Women and Leadership: Selection, Development, Leadership Style, and Performance." *The Journal of Applied Behavioral Science*, 53(1), 32–65.

Table 1	
Company	**Diversity and Inclusion Statement**
Amazon	We are a company of builders who bring varying backgrounds, ideas, and points of view to inventing on behalf of our customers. Our diverse perspectives come from many sources including gender, race, age, national origin, sexual orientation, culture, education, and professional and life experience. We are committed to diversity and inclusion and always look for ways to scale our impact as we grow.
Pinterest	At Pinterest, we're on a mission to bring everyone the inspiration to create a life they love. When we say "everyone," we mean everyone. And when we say "inspiration," we believe that starts with inclusion. For our global workforce (Pinployees) and users (Pinners) to be inspired, we want them to feel safe, welcomed, valued, and respected for their individuality. And to spark creativity, they must be exposed to new ideas, methods, and options. That's why every day at Pinterest, our inclusion and diversity (I&D) work strives for Pinclusion.
McDonald's	We are committed to actively fostering an inclusive environment where diversity is embraced as an advantage. This is a cultural climate that spans the entire McDonald's system. It builds on the work we've done around the world, recognizes where we can continue to make strides, and takes every opportunity to emphasize that inclusion is central to who we are.

Table 1	
Uber Technologies, Inc.	We're committed to increasing demographic diversity at Uber and becoming a more actively antiracist company and ally to the communities we serve. Our executive leadership team is doing their part to make this a reality through setting goals around representation on their teams and tracking progress regularly. In 2020, we also made public antiracist commitments to extend our efforts through our products and our partnerships and to all users on our platform. We actively manage and track these commitments and are progressing on all of them.

Concluding Comments

Clearly diversity work has gotten the mainstream's attention—and there is no denying that we have come a long way since the 1950s when diversity, equity, and inclusion work first started. But we still have a long way to go.

CHAPTER 2

THE NEUROBIOLOGY OF BIAS

Think about the first time you started to understand and recognize the power of differences. Maybe it had to do with "race". Or with gender. Maybe the first time you encountered differences was in relation to your own nationality. Or to someone's level of physical or mental ability. What thoughts were running through your head? What emotions do you recall going through your body?

Now think about the last time you did something new or different. Maybe you tried a new hobby or tried a new culinary experience. What were your thoughts and feelings then? Are they like the ones you felt when you encountered differences for the first time?

My guess is that the answer to the last question is yes and no. On a conscious level, you probably recorded the experience differently as being either more positive or more negative. But on a subcortical level, our emotions are closely linked with our decision-making, and our brain processes all new stimuli in roughly the same manner, regardless of type. Indeed, our neurobiology is the root cause of most of our actions, yet the ways in which the body impacts thoughts, feelings, and behavior is widely misunderstood.

The Mind Versus the Brain

Although often used interchangeably, the mind and brain are two different things. The mind refers to a person's conscious understanding and cognitive thought process, whereas the brain is the organ that is actually responsible for the context in which our conscious understanding and cognitive thought processes are framed. The brain is physical; it can be touched. It is made up of blood vessels and coordinates our movement and feelings. The mind, on the other hand, cannot be touched. It's hypothetical in nature and is not made up of cells. We believe that we respond to the world around us based on our conscious mind's instructions, but actually, at least 90 percent of the time, our conscious mind is responding to our brain's assessment of what is happening around us and in us. The mind deducts reasoning from the decisions instantaneously made by the brain, not the other way around. And our brain's one and only task is to do what is necessary to keep us safe.

From my work with corporations, nonprofits, and government entities, I have learned that most organizations do not understand the way this dynamic works. If they did, they would realize that given our neurobiology, bias is a fundamental part of how we navigate reality. That is, if our brains are healthy, then we have bias. If we can accept that everyone has bias, then we are in a better place to have a conversation around differences. Does that make sense?

The Threat of "New and Different"

When we encounter someone of a different background, the threat of the "new and different" can easily be activated. Decisions of safety are grounded in the fight-or-flight response mechanism. Fight-or-flight is an instantaneous decision that occurs when your brain encounters a stimulus or predicament that it believes might undermine our well-being. At that moment, a decision is made to stand our ground and fight or to flee the scene entirely. (There is also an abundance of research that includes "fawn" and "freeze" as possible reactions as well.)

The brain is highly active in this process. The brain sends adrenaline, cortisol, and other neurochemicals to the large organ groups and shunts blood from our extremities to the core of our body. It is preparing us to actually fight or flee; the context of the situation is not in its safety-first algorithm. Knowing just a little about this sequence can alter the course of our interactions with people toward more productive outcomes. Learning to disrupt this process is at the core of disciplines such as emotional intelligence. If you understand how people are and how they work, you can respond differently to triggers in the external environment that threaten your sense of psychological safety.

Managing Information Overload

Clearly now our conscious minds are secondary players in our decision-making. The common conception though is that we process reality from the top down, that our conscious mind guides our behavior. In a simplified form, we work from the bottom up. We receive information through our brain stem, which then communicates with our amygdala, which ultimately creates those safety-based decisions. Then, and only then, does the conscious mind begin to assign meaning to the stimuli and the chain of events.

When it is functioning at full capacity, our brain has a tremendous task to manage. We receive something like 11 million bits of data per second, but we can only process fifty or so bits per second. Stereotypes are formed out of the need to manage this incoming information. New data is compared to old data and then becomes available for interpretation.

Thus, stereotyping when it comes to human characteristics—whether it's on account of one's race, gender, ethnic origin, age, sexual orientation, religion, and so forth—is merely a rudimentary way of managing information overload and addressing "fear". If we understand that this is the cognitive process that is happening, we can work to disrupt unproductive reactions and impulses toward the "new and different."

The Role of Cognitive Bias

If you look up the definition of *cognitive bias,* it is often called an "execution error". But how can it be called an error if that is how our brain operates? In our culture we refer to a person whose brain lets in whatever new information it encounters as "insane" or "unhealthy" from the Latin. A healthy brain initially screens out new information. If new information is to be incorporated, it is placed into convenient categories based on previous experiences. The brain makes any attempt it can to simplify information processing. To this effect, biases are also tied to memory. Previous experiences with the "new and different" are recalled, as well as the associated emotions.

But while having cognitive bias is normal for a healthy brain, it can also lead to irrational interpretations and judgments. We are all human, so we can all make mistakes. Further, we can be grossly unaware of our biases, which can have detrimental effects on those around us.

How Bias Is Formed

So then, bias is a natural process for humans, and it is rooted in the desire to simplify and make quick decisions around safety. Bias is formed through a series of cognitive processes. In the first phase, visceral, subjective emotions can be observed. In the second phase, that emotion is converted into affective judgments about the situation. Then comes our threat processing: we determine whether the stimulus is friend or foe. In the fourth stage, stereotypes are activated, and in the fifth phase, impressions are formed. In the final phase, we respond.

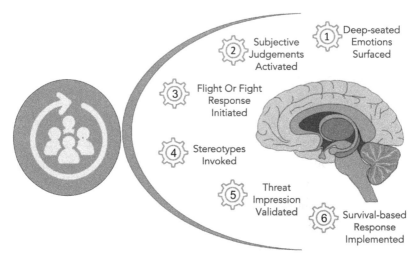

Figure 1. Phases of Bias Formation

At this juncture, it becomes important to understand the difference between responding and reacting. When we respond, we recognize that we have gone through a series of cognitive processes that are designed to help inform our decision-making. Knowing this can help you make better calls when it comes to dealing with similarities and differences. Without some degree of mindfulness our brain will go about its job of "protecting" us and we will simply react.

Implicit Versus Explicit Bias

Bias in organizational settings can manifest itself in both conscious and unconscious ways by means of policies, bylaws, routine procedures, interpersonal interactions, and illegally discriminatory practices that can be deeply rooted in the heart of the organization. To this end, understanding the nature of contemporary forms of bias can guide the development of our strategies and interventions to reduce prejudice in the workplace.

Implicit bias refers to bias that is unconscious, not spoken about, and out of the person's awareness. This type of bias occurs when one is influenced by preexisting beliefs about a certain group of people. Implicit bias is automatically activated, and it can affect judgements, decisions, and behaviors. Thus, these unconscious and hidden biases are often negative associations that people unknowingly hold.

Harvard is well known for its implicit association tests that look at attitudes and beliefs that people may be unwilling or unable to report. These preferences (or aversions) may take on a variety of forms. For example, you may say that you think men and women should be equal in science, but you may associate scientific competence with men more than with women. Or when it comes to ethnicity, you may show a preference for White over Black through your responses to visual stimuli of White/Black images.

Today much of the bias expressed in workplace settings is of the implicit type. Based on my consulting experience, I can comfortably say that a good 80 percent of the bias in organizations is implicit. This is a shift from previous eras when bias was readily expressed in an overt manner. This is explicit bias. Examples of explicit bias may be public statements by management such as "Women are inferior to men" or "African Americans aren't fit for leadership". Explicit bias exists when one is aware of one's preexisting beliefs about a certain group and makes intentional decisions based on those beliefs. Bias of this nature is well within one's awareness and is easy to self-report.

What Really Is Diversity, Equity, and Inclusion?

One of the ways that this effort has been made more difficult is in the way we see DEI itself. The DEI acronym is often used as one construct when in fact it is obviously three different terms. Together, these terms have been widely used by scholars and practitioners alike to talk about differences and the related biases. Diversity, equity, and inclusion are not, however, interchangeable terms. Diversity refers to representation, or the makeup of an entity, whereas equity is about the root causes of bias at the systemic level. Inclusion is about how well diverse perspectives, values, and contributions are integrated into the workplace environment. Creating the term *DEI* and wielding it as if it was a single construct is problematic because the strategies to address each is different. For diversity work, the strategies often lie in the recruitment or selection process, equity work relies on data analysis, whereas inclusion work continues throughout the employee life cycle identifying real and perceived barriers to full participation and that sometimes elusive sense of belonging.

Although the issues are equally egregious regardless of which term you are using, the way we go about diagnosing, normalizing, analyzing, and implementing solutions for each is *very* different.

Today, the term *diversity* is still used as a catchphrase to refer primarily to race/ethnicity and gender. Chalking up diversity to just the obvious categories of difference is a huge missed opportunity as it fails to target other avenues where cultural biases negatively impact productivity. In actuality, diversity can refer to any manner of characteristics including race, ethnicity, age, class, gender, nationality, religion, sexual orientation, or any other demographic factor that describes people, their outlooks and interests. Primary dimensions of diversity tend to be rather observable demographic characteristics that people can use to classify themselves and others.

Of course, the definition of diversity should extend beyond just observable human characteristics. Diversity can also refer to personal experiences that define outcomes, such as educational background, geographical location, occupation, marital status, or birth order (shout out to all of us "only children"!). Or it can refer to personal styles or tendencies, such as when we study differences in conflict-management style, decision-making style, or learning style. Frankly, one of the more significant aspects is what I have labeled "functional" diversity. This is the distinctive culture of a department, a work unit, management, supervision, or front-line workers. An awful lot of productivity falls through these cracks. Generally speaking, the focus of diversity is on identity group factors and the study of group differences.

Equity, a related term, refers to the quality of being fair and impartial and usually in reference to the way services are delivered. At the core of the principles of equity is certainly that all people should be treated equally. However, the practice of equity is often hard—with differential treatment among groups based on access to power and decision-making authority emanating from historical patterns and practices.

Internal to the organization, there may be inequity present in policies and procedures, typically in the human resources dimension. By and large, however, most of the internal DEI issues tend to be around inclusion more so than equity. Equity, however, is a HUGE societal issue and has been for centuries. The disparities in outcomes for certain segments of the African American population for example, —health, income, and education—is at the center of efforts to address racial equity in our society.

Inclusion, the last term of the DEI acronym, simply means, inviting the "other" in. It can also mean fostering diverse perspectives, even if they are counter to the status quo. This is where I have also seen a significant opportunity for most organizations. So much productivity is lost because employees feel disengaged, lack a sense of empowerment, or feel that barriers exist in being able to contribute to the mission.

Throughout my consultations, I have seen time and time again, organizations who throw everything related to diversity in one place; the only member of the executive team who is a person of color is the "DEI manager." Or diversity initiatives are only taken up by racioethnic minority members or women, as if they were the only ones who have ethnicity or gender. Doing so often burdens the very populations you seek to help and support.[13]

Concluding Comments

As I said, most of the work I have seen in diversity, equity, and inclusion makes overcoming our biases harder than it is. You do not need to see a therapist to deliver yourself from biases. If we do a better job of understanding how we are built, then we can begin to exert more influence over our neurobiology. The decision is ours.

---

[13] https://incafrica.com/library/joely-simon-how-to-keep-up-your-anti-racist-work-practices-6-months-after-george-floyds-death.

CHAPTER 3

DIVERSITY AND CULTURAL AWARENESS

Diversity encompasses a wide range of observable and non-observable traits, including gender, race, ethnicity, language, and ability. Additionally, less noticeable differences, such as socioeconomic background, political beliefs, education, work experience, and neurobiology, contribute to the rich tapestry of diversity. Recognizing and appreciating these distinctions is crucial for fostering inclusivity and understanding in our diverse world.In this chapter, we will explore areas of difference in the workplace. This section will also include reflections on my time in practice and observations based on being immersed in diversity work for the past four decades. As with our neurobiology, I believe that if we are aware of the complexity of the various cultural dynamics around us, we can be better prepared to work across, and with, differences.

Before we begin, I'd like you to think about your own identity. What makes up your universe of differences? In what ways are you like those around you? In what ways are you different? What social identity groups carry the most meaning for you? As we dive deeper into exploring the universe of differences, keep these questions about yourself in mind. Knowing your own frame of reference is critical in discovering and learning about differences. There is much truth to the critique of DEI that you can end up spending too much time on differences rather than on finding common ground. The goal is to appreciate that our similarities are what count the most. However, because of the difficult histories that are part and parcel of our experience, our differences can present an initial barrier. The idea then is that if we can overcome those barriers with a better understanding of the impact of culture, we enable ourselves to celebrate and leverage both similarities and differences. Here is a depiction of this universe that I like to see as an "onion," each layer revealing another dimension. Traditionally, this has been developed with the notion of that which is most readily observable down toward those aspects of a person that may be least observable. That approach fails us miserably in our current cultural complexity, but I'll stick with the idea just to make the illustration easier. I've also added the dimension of "functional diversity" in an organization so that the full breadth of diversity is captured.

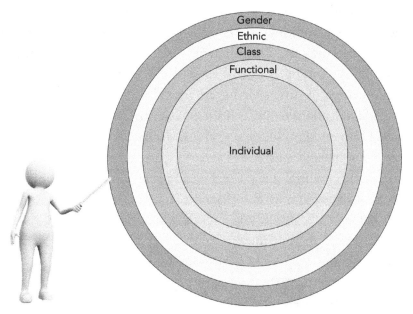

Figure 2. The Universe of Differences

In the workplace, the two observable human characteristics that get the most attention are gender and race/ethnicity. Children as young as three can accurately apply gender labels to themselves and others. By the age of five, children develop the capacity to apply racial/ ethnic labels to themselves and others—a process that is learned even earlier by children from ethnic minorities.[14] Indeed, from a young age, we are socialized to understand that different gender and racial/ethnic groups exist and that we belong to one or more of them.

While today a spectrum exists when it comes to gender, in Western cultures, gender is normally categorized along the binary dimensions of female/male or woman/man. However, modern definitions of gender tend to be more inclusive and speak more to gender *identity* rather than sex assigned at birth. This distinction allows for more fluid definitions of gender to occur (e.g., nonbinary and transgender). Gender is just as much a sociocultural process as it is biological. At a young age, gender conditioning begins. Boys were historically encouraged to participate in activities that emphasize dominance and competitiveness. Girls, on the other hand, were historically encouraged to engage in communal behavior that exhibits warmth, connection, and interaction. Consequently, when it comes to gender, stereotypes are formed about what is acceptable, desirable, and expected behavior for each group.

We also become acutely aware of race and/or ethnicity. Each country has its own set of ethnic groups. In the United States, the most common racioethnic groups include African Americans, Asian Americans, European Americans, Hispanic Americans, and Native Americans, to name a few.[15] However, America, like much of the world, is rapidly diversifying, bringing new meaning to the terms and even more diversity when it comes to race/ethnicity. In the last 10-12

---

[14] Rogers, L. O., and Meltzoff, A. N. (2017). "Is Gender More Important and Meaningful than Race? An Analysis of Racial and Gender Identity among Black, White, and Mixed-Race Children." *Cultural Diversity and Ethnic Minority Psychology*, 23(3), 323.

[15] Roberson, L., and Block, C. J. (2001). "Racioethnicity and Job Performance: A Review and Critique of Theoretical Perspectives on the Causes of Group Differences." *Research in Organizational Behavior,* 23, 247–325.

years there has been an exponential increase in individuals identifying as biracial or multiracial. Like gender, race/ethnicity also plays an important role in the perceptions that others have of us. In many cases, our racioethnic membership can dictate and impact a variety of outcomes—both in the workplace and within society writ large.

After gender and racioethnicity, the next most common variable of difference is class, that is growing up lower, middle, upper-middle, upper class, and so on. Socioeconomic status (or SES for short) is a combination of education, income, and occupation. In this way, it is an amalgam of tangible and intangible measures. Few areas of life exist that are not impacted by class. Links between socioeconomic class and education,[16] health,[17] and housing[18] have been well documented in the United States and abroad.

Your socioeconomic class dictates your social habits, which makes it so that we may often have as much in common with people who are in our income brackets, educational levels, and professional circles, as those who are from our own identified racioethnic group. Oftentimes, within gender groups or within racioethnic groups, class can really be the distinguishing characteristic. It may also be the case that class can subvert the negative effects of race. In a seminal study looking at race-class stereotypes, psychologists at Howard University found that both upper-class Whites and Blacks were described as *intelligent, ambitious, industrious, neat, and progressive.*[19] In 1956, when this study

[16] Bicer, A., Capraro, M. M., and Capraro, R. (2013). "The Effects of Parent's SES and Education Level on Students' Mathematics Achievement: Examining the Mediation Effects of Parental Expectations and Parental Communication." *The Online Journal of New Horizons in Education*, 3(4), 89–97.

[17] Veenstra, G. (2000). "Social Capital, SES and Health: An Individual-Level Analysis." *Social Science & Medicine*, 50(5), 619–629.

[18] Fang, M., Mirutse, G., Guo, L., and Ma, X. (2019). "Role of Socioeconomic Status and Housing Conditions in Geriatric Depression in Rural China: A Cross-Sectional Study." *BMJ Open*, 9(5), e024046.

[19] Bayton, J. A., McAlister, L. B., and Hamer, J. (1956). "Race-Class Stereotypes." *The Journal of Negro Education*, 25(1), 75–78.

was conducted, you can imagine that the same could not be said for lower-class Blacks. Thus, class can impact how others see us, and consequently treat us, in profound ways.

The trifecta of race, gender, and class, often informs the lived experiences of people in more prolific ways than examining these variables of differences in silos. The term *intersectionality* was developed by Kimberlé Crenshaw in 1989 to describe the lived experiences of those who exist on the margins of society. Key to intersectionality is the idea of dual subordination. That is, due to being in a position of dual subordination—first maybe by your race/ethnicity, and then perhaps by your gender or class—you have increased the likelihood of invisibility in the discourse, perspective, or experience. Given this, intersectionality scholars call for the study of not only gender, race, or class but the overall combination. Much of the impactful work in racial equity seeks to address the trifecta impact of systemic bias based on one's gender, race, AND class.

Countless studies in the social sciences have documented the effects of intersectionality on a range of outcomes including compensation,[20] upward mobility,[21] and advancement potential.[22] Using an intersectionality lens allows for greater nuances to be explored within and among gender and racioethnic groups. Indeed, an intersectionality approach prevents treating membership in a certain group as a monolithic experience. This term also implies that looking at the combination of gender, racioethnicity, and class—and the associated isms together (i.e., sexism, racism, and classism) is again more impactful than examining these areas of difference alone.

Diversity is not always located at the human demographic level.

---

[20] Keene, K. P., and Jenks, C. (2022). "The Role of Identity Intersectionality in Compensation Inequity within Anesthesia." *Anesthesia & Analgesia*, 135(1), e3.

[21] Romero, M., and Valdez, Z. (2016). "Introduction to the Special Issue: Intersectionality and Entrepreneurship." *Ethnic and Racial Studies*, 39(9), 1553–1565.

[22] Smooth, W. G. (2016). "Intersectionality and Women's Advancement in the Discipline and across the Academy." *Politics, Groups, and Identities*, 4(3), 513–528.

Indeed, diversity can also be related to a "functional" grouping that is tied to your occupation, department or work unit, particular job duties, where you sit in the org chart, etc. In the past, I have consulted with many organizations where the various functions operated and indeed acted, as if they were part of separate entities. The culture between Sales and IT or between Human Resources and Accounting could not be more different. Thus, one's organizational role can also be a measure of difference and impact outcomes, such as creativity[23] or team cohesion.[24]

The research is mixed on the relationship between functional diversity and team effectiveness.[25] Some studies have found that functionally-diverse management teams respond better to competitive threats,[26] develop clearer strategies,[27] and are more innovative[28] than nonfunctionally-diverse teams. However, other studies have found that being on heterogeneous teams in terms of functional differences can impede performance due to an increase in conflict and differences

---

[23] Zhang, Y. (2016). "Functional Diversity and Group Creativity: The Role of Group Longevity." *The Journal of Applied Behavioral Science*, 52(1), 97–123.

[24] Post, C. (2015). "When Is Female Leadership an Advantage? Coordination Requirements, Team Cohesion, and Team Interaction Norms." *Journal of Organizational Behavior*, 36(8), 1153–1175.

[25] Bunderson, J. S., and Sutcliffe, K. M. (2002). "Comparing Alternative Conceptualizations of Functional Diversity in Management Teams: Process and Performance Effects." *Academy of Management Journal*, 45(5), 875–893.

[26] Hambrick, D. C., Cho, T. S., and Chen, M. J. (1996). "The Influence of Top Management Team Heterogeneity on Firms' Competitive Moves." *Administrative Science Quarterly*, 659–684.

[27] Bantel, K. A. (1993). "Strategic Clarity in Banking: Role of Top Management-Team Demography." *Psychological Reports*, 73(3_suppl), 1187–1201.

[28] Cheung, S. Y., Gong, Y., Wang, M., Zhou, L., and Shi, J. (2016). "When and How Does Functional Diversity Influence Team Innovation? The Mediating Role of Knowledge Sharing and the Moderation Role of Affect-Based Trust in a Team." *Human Relations*, 69(7), 1507–1531.

of opinion/perspective.[29] Authority level can also be another lever of diversity in workgroups and systems. In organizations that have a strict hierarchy (e.g., many US government agency offices, the military, large nonprofits, and many "Fortune 500s"), the differences in lived experience between individual contributors, middle managers, and senior leadership can be vast. I refer to this as the "undiscovered country" of diversity and inclusion. I feel comfortable saying again that A LOT of productivity is lost in organizations because of the dysfunctional cultural interaction between executives/managers/supervisors and the so-called "working level" of the organization. I can say objectively that the patriarchal mentality in many workplaces absolutely destroys any sense of belonging, inclusion, or psychological safety as you go deeper into the ranks.

Taken together, the studies provide evidence that diversity is not always "skin deep" and can manifest itself in any number of ways. Differences can even exist when it comes to the way in which we work best and operate most efficiently. Our energy levels may also be active at different times throughout the day. When it comes to performance, this may mean that you have a preference to do your work at a particular time of day. Some people may prefer to work in the morning, while others may prefer to work at night. While generally having a less drastic effect on organizational dynamics in comparison to gender, race, and class, our biological processes can still impact workplace dynamics and are certainly included in the universe of differences. One of the lessons learned during the COVID period was that overall productivity soared as organizations quickly pivoted to working virtually. That patriarchal culture that resisted telework for so many years had to finally give way. Leadership discovered that employees could in fact be trusted to work even when they weren't able to "watch them." They found out that those who were surfing

---

[29] Peters, L., and Karren, R. J. (2009). "An Examination of the Roles of Trust and Functional Diversity on Virtual Team Performance Ratings." *Group & Organization Management*, 34(4), 479–504.

the web and playing Solitaire had been doing it when we were all in the office as well!

Another way that we differ of course is in our personality. By now, you have probably heard of the Myers-Briggs Type Indicator or the MBTI. The Myers-Briggs categorizes people on the dichotomous scales of extroversion/introversion, sensing/intuition, thinking/feeling, and judging/perceiving. Based on your personality preferences, each person is assigned a four-letter personality type that provides insight into your preferences. The MBTI dichotomies are just one example of how people's personality characteristics can impact where we get our energy from, how we take in information, how we make decisions, and ultimately, how we organize our world. Our personalities can impact a range of outcomes and thus are an important indicator to pay attention to in groups and organizational settings.

Another personality assessment that is popular in organizational settings is the DiSC, which can help teams and groups improve teamwork, communication, and productivity. DiSC is an acronym that stands for dominance, influence, conscientiousness, and steadiness. Each of these styles represents behavioral tendencies and consequently can impact how groups and teams function. Again, understanding that some team members may prefer dominance, while another may prefer influence for example, may be telling in a wide variety of contexts. My one admonition would be to not take these assessment instruments too far. They represent preferences that we can act outside of on a regular basis if we so choose or need to.

Diversity: Most Organizations Have Plenty

So, when it comes to diversity, do organizations have enough? The short answer is yes. If that is the case, then why are some companies still talking about instituting hiring quotas or engaging in affirmative action hiring? Why do institutions need internal diversity officers? Why is diversity *still* a buzzword even in a "post-racial" society?

As mentioned, while the United States labor force is diverse, much of the gender and racioethnic diversity is concentrated at the lower levels of the organization. Indeed, in many organizations, the demographics of the workplace do not mirror the demographics of leadership or the ones making decisions. In many instances, especially in high-paying industries, women and individuals of color do not make it past middle management. A study conducted by Deloitte found that only 1.2 percent of CEOs of "Fortune 500" companies are Black, a number that fails in comparison to 13.5 percent,[30] which is the percentage of Black workers in the United States. Women make up just 8.8 percent of "Fortune 500" CEOs, which is drastically short of 47 percent, the percentage of women workers in America.

Again, it may be helpful to highlight the distinction between diversity and inclusion. Remember that diversity is being invited to the party. Inclusion is being asked to dance. Today, most everyone is welcome to take a place in the workforce. However, not everyone has an equal opportunity of advancing or even being adequately rewarded for their efforts. And in some extreme cases, many don't even get to hear the music playing.

In today's workplace, especially at the upper echelons of leadership, inclusion is both a major issue and a major opportunity, especially for members who may not share the gender, racioethnic, or class grouping of the organizational founders or decision-makers. Given that most American founders and organizational leaders are male[31] and White,[32] this has posed challenges for women and people of color. While not always explicit, bias is alive and well in today's institutions.

---

[30] https://www2.deloitte.com/content/dam/Deloitte/us/Documents/center-for-board-effectiveness/missing-pieces-fortune-500-board-diversity-study-6th-edition-report.pdf.

[31] Gipson et al., 2017.

[32] Roberson and Block, 2001.

Clearly when it comes to being inclusive at the highest levels, most organizations have a long way to go. Organizations that have really embraced inclusion have identified the precise point in the hierarchy where gender and ethnic diversity begin to fade.

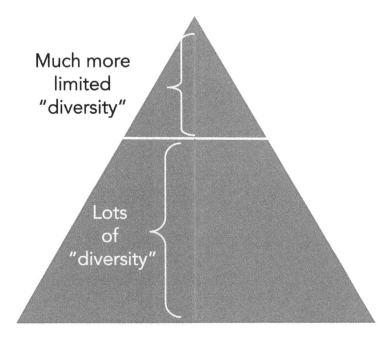

Figure 3. Organizational Diversity

Those "above the line" are connected to the bright, up-and-coming folks "below the line" where both formal and informal mentoring, shadowing, coaching, project participation, or short-term details allow for the definition of "people like me" to be recast.

Recruiting and Retention

Sometimes, lack of diversity is due to other contextual or environmental factors. I have consulted with John Deere, an American corporation that manufactures agriculture and lawn care equipment.

The headquarters of the company is in Moline, Illinois. Because most of the corporate offices are also in more rural locations, the company has difficulty recruiting ethnic minorities as most ethnic groups live in urban areas. Diversity can greatly impact your recruitment and retention efforts. For example, when it comes to careers in Fire and Rescue, it can be hard to get people from certain Asian backgrounds to enlist. If they align with Buddhist culture, they may subscribe to a different cultural archetype around fire and therefore are less inclined to go into firefighting and related fields. In other cultures, the concept of "rescue" is drastically different. Of course, these examples assume that a particular individual's values align with the cultural archetype, but I hope you get the main point here.

To successfully recruit, it is important to go to diverse labor markets that are known for turning out high-quality talent. Reliance on traditional avenues of recruitment can pose challenges for organizations looking to diversify. What is important is to recruit, not to fill quotas, but to find high-level talent. For example, in the Black community, at historically Black colleges and universities (i.e., HBCUs), sororities and fraternities play a powerful role in terms of finding top talent. True, HBCUs have lower graduation rates than their predominately White institution counterparts; however, these lower rates are based mainly on economics not intelligence. Once you understand that, you discover that HBCUs can be a fertile recruiting ground for companies looking to recruit and retain high-potential workers. In fact, the investment in the STEM fields at places like Prairie View A&M, Spelman, Alabama A&M, North Carolina A&T, Morgan, Hampton, Howard, or Florida A&M has produced a deep pool of talent. Yet few companies expand their efforts beyond traditional recruitment avenues.

Finding a talented and a diverse source of employees requires a little bit of give-and-take. Underrepresented groups must be willing to be initial trailblazers, and organizations must overcome their biases when it comes to certain recruiting grounds. Further, when it comes to recruiting, it is also important to maintain fair hiring practices throughout the hiring cycle. Remember different is not always difficult.

Issues of Upward Mobility, Promotion, Advancement, and Compensation

Societally, upward mobility is the act of moving to a higher social class or acquiring increased wealth or status. In the workplace, upward mobility is the act of moving from one position to a higher-ranking position that carries more authority and responsibility. Upward mobility, and the related terms of promotion and advancement, can be tricky for women, racioethnic minority members, and lower-ranked professionals. The term *glass ceiling* has been widely used to describe the experiences of women and racioethnic minority members as they attempt to climb the corporate ladder. The glass ceiling refers to invisible barriers that prevent the advancement of underrepresented groups to senior management. It is said that in some industries, the ceiling is more like concrete.

Issues with compensation are a by-product of not focusing on upward mobility, promotion, and advancement. When it comes to wages, the gender gap is well documented in the popular press and in the empirical literature. American women on average make $0.82 to every $1 earned by American men.[33] Greater wage discrepancies have been found in fields that have been historically male dominated, such as academia, business, and medicine.[34] As male-dominated industries typically carry higher wages than female-dominated industries, these

---

[33] Catalyst (March 2020). *"Women's Earnings: The Pay Gap: Quick Take."* New York, NY: Catalyst. Retrieved from https://www.catalyst.org/research/womens-earnings-the-pay-gap/.

[34] Gipson, A. N. (2021). "The Impact of Dual Stereotype Threat and Power on Negotiation Behavior and Affect." Columbia University.

findings are troubling for female workers, especially in high-profile careers.

The difference in income largely stems from the fact that women, and especially women of color, have been historically stratified in lower paying occupations than their male counterparts. Even within occupations, differences exist. For example, women physicians tend to be concentrated in lower-paying specialties like pediatrics and general surgery and make nearly $17,000 less than even their newly minted male counterparts.[35]

Once again, even though women make up nearly half of the workforce, this representation does not translate into movement into the upper echelons of leadership. Studies show that women are promoted at a slower rate than their male counterparts in a variety of different fields and industries. The terms *glass labyrinth,* and *titanium ceiling* have also been used to describe the experiences of women attempting to climb the corporate ladder. As positions of leadership generally come with higher-paying jobs, the underrepresentation of women in leadership has significant economic effects.

Labor statistics also show discrepancies in wages across racioethnic groups. Asian Americans and European Americans far outstrip their African American and Hispanic American counterparts when it comes to average weekly wages. According to the United States Bureau of Labor Statistics,[36] the average Asian American makes $1,174 per week, the average European American makes $945 per week, whereas the average African American makes just $735 per week, and the average Hispanic American earns just $706 per week (figure 4). Women of all racioethnic groups make less than their male counterparts.

---

[35] Lo Sasso, A. T., Richards, M. R., Chou, C. F., and Gerber, S. E. (2011). "The $16,819 Pay Gap for Newly Trained Physicians: The Unexplained Trend of Men Earning More than Women." *Health Affairs*, 30(2), 193–201.

[36] US Bureau of Labor Statistics (2019). "Median Weekly Earnings for Full-Time Wage and Salary Workers by Selected Characteristics." Retrieved from https://www.bls.gov/cps/ cpsaat37.pdf.

Again, these numbers are largely reflective of the fact that women and people of color are generally situated at the lower rungs of organizational structures.

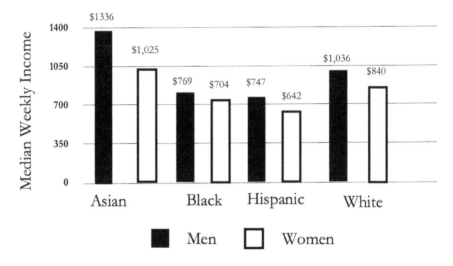

Figure 4. The Gender and Racioethnic Wage Gaps

Concluding Comments

This chapter sought to further explore the ways in which the universe of differences impacts important workplace related outcomes. To this end, this section provided an overview of the key variables of difference when it comes to people, introduced the idea of intersectionality, and discussed the outcomes of various underrepresented groups in the workplace, specifically in relation to upward mobility, promotion, advancement, and compensation. This section also hoped to highlight the importance of examining variables of difference in conjunction with one another, to present a more dynamic picture.

CHAPTER 4

THE QUEST FOR EQUITY

Have you ever heard the fable *Building a House for Diversity* written by DEI scholar and pioneer Dr. Roosevelt Thomas Jr.?[37] The story features two animals: a giraffe and an elephant. In this fable, the giraffe lives in a beautiful family home designed especially for giraffes. The high windows, narrow hallways, and dainty staircase pose no challenges for the family of tall, slender mammals. The giraffe loved his house and thought it was close to perfect.

One day, the giraffe's friend, the elephant, came to visit. From the beginning, the elephant had trouble navigating the giraffe's house. It was hard for him to fit into the front door; the giraffe had to open a second panel to let him in. At one point, the elephant wanted to go upstairs. However, when he put his weight on the stairs, he heard them crack. The giraffe suggested that the elephant lose some weight; if only he were smaller, everything would be better.

Disheveled, the elephant took a pause. It didn't seem like the giraffe was being very understanding. Instead of acknowledging the limitations of the house he built, the giraffe told the elephant to fix

---

[37] Thomas, R. R., and Woodruff, M. I. (1999). *Building a House for Diversity.* New York: AMACOM.
Chicago.

himself. What was clear was that a house that was built for a giraffe would need some major changes if it were to work for an elephant.

This fable illustrates how too often systems—organizations, companies, groups, teams, etc.—are built with the founders in mind and not necessarily "others." While like-minded individuals tend to do well in such a culture, those who have opposing or different perspectives can be ostracized or even marginalized within the dominant culture. The story is a powerful lesson of the intersections between diversity, equity, and change. It is also helpful starting point for our chapter on the quest for equity. I must admit that when I read Thomas' fable, I can see how it's not fair to suggest that the giraffe build a dwelling for personal habitation that must fit others who do not have to live there. The fable's real power is when you apply it to organizations which by definition are designed to house a diverse collection of skills, capabilities, and personalities.

Uncovering the Cause of Systemic Bias

Equity is a major social issue and can also surface within organizations. The difficult thing in DEI has been the confluence of the two domains. The quest for equity starts with uncovering the causes of systemic biases that produce disparate outcomes for society and can extend to the workplace. As mentioned in the previous chapter, for a lot of employees, it can be hard to climb the corporate ladder, due to both real and invisible barriers. If we are to disrupt bias from impacting outcomes, we must first look at the antecedents and the underlying causes of the differential treatment in the first place.

Racism, sexism, and even to some extent classism, can be at the root of many disparate outcomes for underrepresented groups. However, it can be difficult to solve a problem if there is a lack of awareness that a problem even exists. For example, did you know that the majority of White Americans believe that anti-White sentiment is on the increase and anti-Black sentiment is on the decrease?[38] In fact, according to research, most White Americans (57 percent) believe anti-White racism is a bigger problem than anti-Black racism, a notion not supported by recent Black perspectives.

Again, bias is not always explicit. Sometimes, it is the implicit kind that can do the most damage. If people do not know that they are biased, it can be hard to genuinely engage in problem solving around meaningful solutions. Remember, *people* oversee *systems*. Biases that individuals had one hundred years ago become systemic and baked into organizations. It may be that your company only recruits from the most selective universities in America, which historically have had low representations of racioethnic minority members. Or perhaps promotion is based on a referral system that is biased toward those most like the leadership team. Equity's role is to uncover the underlying causes of that bias and address it.

Systemic bias may be rooted in several dimensions of organizational operations, and again, it may not be always easy to identify. Thus, knowing that our neurobiology is wired for bias can be a helpful start. And indeed, bias has shown up in almost every major system in America including housing, education, economic development, and healthcare. In housing, redlining makes it so that many people of color have trouble qualifying for loans in well-to-do areas. In healthcare, Black patients are treated differently from White patients based on biased algorithms. In the workplace, digital hiring platforms may reject resumes from individuals with nontraditional names before it even reaches a person. Bias is everywhere, and it is not going away.

Equity seeks to level the playing field. The goal is for ethnicity (or gender or class) not to determine your future. Right now, for a lot of people, your ethnicity can be the major predictor for all sorts of outcomes and life trajectories. The hope is that if we work toward building equitable systems, this will cease to be the case. If we are to

---

[38] Livingston, R. (2020). "How to Promote Racial Equity in the Workplace." *Harvard Business Review*, 98(5), 64–72.

change our systems, our workplace policies and procedures must be readjusted. Stereotyping in organizational contexts and institutional settings needs to be addressed. Further, preferential bias toward in-group members and illegally discriminatory bias against out-group members also needs to be overcome.

A Complex and Complicated History

When it comes to achieving racial equity, the United States has a long way to go. We have a deep and complicated history with "race", particularly as it relates to African Americans. Racial inequity for African Americans is largely a by-product of enslavement, a devastating time period in the United States characterized by involuntary servitude, violence, cruelty, and oppression. The system of slavery itself was complex, with different ranking and statuses afforded based on skill or skin tone. Vestiges of the effects of slavery are still alive and well today. If one's life experience has not included contact and interaction with African Americans, this can be difficult to concur with.

Most of the 12 million Africans involved with the Atlantic Slave Trade were sent to South America and the Caribbean. Only 6 percent were sent to North America, or roughly half a million. After slavery was dismantled and enslaved people were emancipated in 1863, a new era of Black Codes and Jim Crow laws set in. Today, you might say that a type of "neo-slavery" still exists in the form of institutions such as corrections, where 38 percent of people who are locked up identify as Black or African American. Overlooked by many is the precise language of the 13th amendment related to the abolition of slavery. It says that *"Neither slavery nor involuntary servitude, except as a punishment for crime whereof the party shall have been duly convicted, shall exist within the United States, or any place subject to their jurisdiction"*. It's the "except as punishment for a crime" that has equity advocates more than mildly concerned. Today, our relationship with "race" is just a complex and complicated as it ever was before.

In our society today, at least two generations of workers were not around during the civil rights movement whereby they would have a better understanding of that history. Indeed, if you don't know how bad it was, it can be easy to sweep the experiences of people of color under the rug. If we are to move forward, we need to accept the lessons from our past. Further, if we are to truly conquer our history as it relates to "race", we must not be afraid to confront our past head-on, even if it means having uncomfortable conversations about privilege, access, and mobility.

Internalized Oppression

Indeed the trauma of slavery is still alive and well and can be passed from one generation to the next. I know that it is a harrowing thought, but researchers are confirming its reality across the board. Folks like Cornell's Dr. Chris Mason; Yael Danieli, PhD, cofounder and director of the Group Project for Holocaust Survivors and Their Children in New York; Canadian psychiatrist Vivian M. Rakoff, MD; and Rachel Yehuda, a Professor of Psychiatry and Neuroscience, the Vice Chair for Veterans Affairs in the Psychiatry Department and the Director of the Traumatic Stress Studies Division at the Mount Sinai School of Medicine are at the forefront. This kind of trauma has an *epigenetic* impact, not genetic. Epigenetics looks at how your environment and resulting behaviors can impact the way your genes operate. Epigenetic changes can be mitigated and do not interfere with your DNA sequencing but can affect which genes get "turned on" or not. Trauma can create this effect which can then be passed down to future generations. Again, this is not a genetic mutation, but a significant factor in the expression of one's genes. Our socioeconomic environment has a huge impact on the likelihood of epigenetic trauma. A significant number of African Americans are in the same socioeconomic situation as their great-great-grandparents. Of course, trauma does not care about your social status, but the fewer resources you have, the greater the number and degree of chronic stressors you are likely to experience. This phenomenon is not only centered in the Black community. Great-great grandchildren of Confederate prisoners of war can also carry a high degree of trauma, as can the descendants of Holocaust survivors. In many organizational systems, racial discrimination, or the differential treatment or evaluation based solely on "race", is present. Racial discrimination is prevalent in today's organizational systems and occurs more often than you might think. Sometimes bias is located above the surface, but other times, bias is deeply rooted in the very systems we are trying to change. In recent decades, great strides have been made by scholars and practitioners alike to address illegal discrimination head-on. First, organizational leaders and members must understand the underlying causes. Effective interventions then must seek to develop genuine concern for the "other" and then identify avenues for correction.

Racial prejudice and bigotry emerge through many psychological sources from cognitive biases to ideological preferences to personality characteristics. But racism is largely the outcome of mostly structural factors—laws, procedures, and norms that can encourage, and reward, illegally discriminatory behavior. Often, organizational strategists treat the symptoms of biased processes without addressing the structural foundation that perpetuates the problem. Think about the story of the giraffe and elephant. The giraffe's first impulse was for the elephant to fix himself. At no point was there any mention of how the house that was built may not be inclusive for all. Instead, the elephant, like many racioethnic minorities, must adapt or perish.

Data-Driven Metrics

Internal and external equity practitioners engage several methods to uncover disparities and improve organizational systems. Metrics can take on a variety of forms and may not always be direct measures. The most effective are grounded in quantitative data that is observable and measurable. For example, if organizations are interested in creating parity, they might focus on the workforce mix and compare the organizations' demographics to national demographics. You might look at whether the number of harassment lawsuits has declined or whether costs have been reduced due to lower turnover rates. Or perhaps after instituting diversity in your board do you receive more qualified job applications, higher levels of customer loyalty, or higher productivity and profitability levels? Using various tools to help track your progress can help you benchmark, as well as showcase, progress toward important outcomes.

As an organizational decision-maker, you might also look at offer/acceptance ratios showing how many offers to underrepresented groups were accepted. You might collect data regarding retention, turnover intentions of populations of interest, and track the data over time.

From an external point of view, disparities in service delivery can only be uncovered with data. For many organizations across the sectors this is an important aspect of addressing equity. I've had the honor of supporting Arlington, Virginia, in their equity efforts. The County had developed a focus on equity as early as 2016. The genuineness of its efforts is largely based on the fact they did not just jump on the bandwagon in 2020 and 2021. The Department of Human Services (DHS) is one example. It is headed by a brilliant (and appropriately feisty) Director, Anita Freidman. She supervises all five operational divisions delivering services that promote a community of healthy, safe, and economically secure children, adults, and families. DHS is digging into the data to discover why the same behavioral health services produced different results in the more affluent and less ethnically diverse northern part of the County than in the extremely diverse southern Arlington neighborhoods. It's not an issue of individual prejudice; it's a systemic problem, and Anita and her staff are making amazing progress in getting down to the root cause.

My experience serving the Midwest Energy Efficiency Alliance (MEEA) is another case in point. MEEA is a collaborative network, promoting energy efficiency to optimize energy generation, reduce consumption, create jobs, and decrease carbon emissions in all Midwest communities. Their mission around DEI is to promote commitment "to developing, supporting, and promoting innovative and impactful policies and actions to strengthen the energy efficiency industry by prioritizing equity, inclusion, access, and diversity." Who would think there are disparities issues in the energy field? However, "energy justice" is a nationwide effort to uncover and correct the impact of racism, etc. MEEA has accepted the responsibility for moving its members forward. They are tackling problems tied to the fact that residential energy use represents roughly 17% of annual greenhouse gas emissions in the United States. Studies show that legacy housing policies and financial lending practices have negatively impacted housing quality and home ownership in non-Caucasian and immigrant communities. Both factors are key determinants of household energy use. But to date there has been no analysis on a national scale of how race and ethnicity affect household energy use and related carbon emissions. Per capita emissions are higher in historically White neighborhoods than in historically Black neighborhoods, even though the former constitutes more energy-efficient homes (low energy use intensity). This emissions paradox is explained by differences in building age, rates of home ownership, and floor area in these communities. In historically Black neighborhoods, homes are older, home ownership is lower (reducing the likelihood of energy retrofits), and there is less floor area per person compared to historically White neighborhoods. These kinds of problems are indeed exceptional, and it is clear that inequity is at the root. The key will always be getting the data.

Another sterling client example is the National Institute For Automotive Service Excellence (ASE). You likely know more about ASE than you think. You've probably seen their logo at your local mechanic's shop. Since 1972 the independent nonprofit organization has worked to improve the quality of vehicle repair and service by testing and certifying automotive professionals. President and CEO Tim Zilke has put the organization and, indirectly, the nearly 250,000 service professionals it impacts, on a path to use DEI to create an even more inclusive and productive industry. The fact that the industry has gender disparities should be obvious based on the traditional characterization of the field. The "grease monkey" stereotype is far from the truth of what it takes to do the job in the digital age. That is only one of several other messages that Tim and his colleagues are broadcasting to change the face of the industry and open up opportunities for more women to participate. Tim knows that creating an inclusive climate must go together with breaking down the barriers to recruitment as well. In fact, the automotive industry as a whole has been doing some outstanding work. I've had conversations with auto companies, OEMs, aftermarket entities, and automotive suppliers and many are pretty far down the DEI road. BMW, Subaru, Ford, Daimler, Volkswagen are all notable examples. Like ASE, the Center for Automotive Diversity, Inclusion & Advancement (CADIA) is also providing outstanding thought leadership and resources. Cheryl Thompson, CADIA's CEO is a pioneer. She's a veteran of the industry, with career experience at Ford and American Axle and Manufacturing in positions ranging from tool and die, operations, manufacturing engineering and global leadership. Cheryl says" I define diversity as all the things that are visible and invisible that make us different. Most people think of gender, race, ethnicity, and sexual orientation when they hear the word diversity. But it's so much more. It can include age, parental status, family status, and religious or spiritual beliefs. It could be your political views. It could be your educational background. Equity is about giving people what they need to succeed in our industry. We need to evolve that thinking because not everybody has the same needs. Not everybody has the same access. Then inclusion is being able to leverage all those differences".

Focus on Process Reengineering

When it comes to initiating and sustaining equity efforts in the workplace, it can be a difficult process. To change workplace climate, big shifts must be made as it relates to culture and leadership. One key avenue of change is focusing on process reengineering. As organizational decision-makers, it is important to address the systems that can leverage equity such as the processes for staffing, compensation, performance management, etc. Attention should also be paid to the promotion and advancement processes. Membership in a particular identity group should not impact your rate of promotion. On the flip side, finally improving cumbersome, duplicative, and just-plain-broken processes can cast equity efforts in an incredibly favorable light. Since the days of Total Quality Management (TQM) in the 1980's, many of us consultants have been sounding like that proverbial broken record when it comes to the importance of fixing organizational processes. Here again, an incredible amount of productive time and energy gets sucked up by having to operate through antiquated and inefficient systems.

So, what else can organizations do to reveal and correct disparities? Of course, the obvious answer is to not make decisions based off demographic variables. For hiring, why not do a blind review whereby the person's name and gender is removed from the application? Because honestly, what difference does a name make? Or gender? Indeed, for most jobs, gender does not matter. There is a fascinating example of this from the field of classical music. Believe it or not, there has been a long history of gender and ethnic bias in orchestras. Women were not accepted into mainstream orchestra until 1913 as there was deep-seated bias against their participation. In the 1950's the Boston Symphony made a conscientious effort to encourage more women to audition. To attempt to remove the impact of implicit (and explicit) bias, they held "blind auditions" with the candidate entering the room and performing behind a screen. Surprisingly the selection results still ended up overwhelmingly favoring men. Here's where the process engineering concept comes into play. In the 1950's what could possibly distinguish someone's gender as they entered the room for an orchestra audition?........ You got it! Their shoes! Women would be more inclined to wear heels in a formal setting and the clicking sound registered either consciously or subliminally with the predominantly male audition panel. When the musicians were instructed to remove their shoes before entering the room more than half of the women were successful and moved onto the next stage. As far as ethnic bias in this field is concerned, only 2% of orchestra musicians are "people of color" . If we can change our decision-making algorithms, we may have a better chance of disrupting bias in our organizational systems. Lastly, when it comes to reengineering systems, do not be afraid to have tough conversations. Get personal, get real, and grow.

Crafting A Successful Equity Effort

So far, we have discussed why focusing on diversity, equity, and inclusion is an important goal for any organization. The question now is this: if addressing equity is the priority how do you structure it? Most equity efforts begin because systemic disparities have already been identified but nothing has been done to address them. For example, the presence of racial disparities in healthcare, education, or economic development is widely known as it has been a systemic issue for generations. The other scenario is when you want to first gather data to determine whether inequity is present or not. This is naturally a more elongated process. To gather data and identify potential equity issues, start by defining your research question and key variables. Conduct a thorough literature review to understand existing knowledge in the area. Choose appropriate data sources, ensuring they align with your research focus, and request access or permissions as needed. Collect demographic information to allow for intersectional analysis and assess data quality for reliability. If necessary, employ surveys, interviews, or other qualitative methods to capture nuanced experiences. Utilize quantitative analysis to identify patterns and disparities. Consider the geographic context and engage stakeholders throughout the process, incorporating their perspectives. Document your methodology transparently, interpret findings in the context of your research question, and communicate results effectively. This iterative process ensures a comprehensive understanding of equity issues, guiding informed decision-making and targeted interventions for meaningful change.

Once you have established a focus the equity journey can be viewed as three key phases that if handled properly can ensure that disparities are uncovered, and corrective measures identified and implemented. Indeed, with any equity initiative, you will first need to **normalize** the idea of addressing bias, collect and **analyze/prioritize** the data, and then **implement** solutions. A summary of the model and the steps within each phase is presented below.

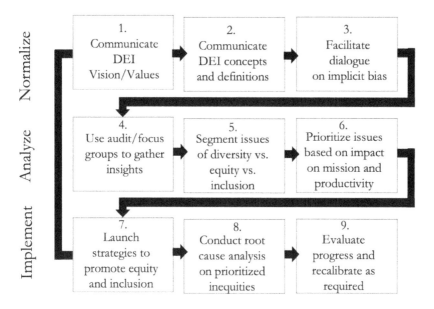

Figure 5. The Three Phases of Successful Equity Efforts

Phase 1: Normalize the Conversation

The goal of the first phase is to normalize the concept of bias. As mentioned in chapter 2, bias, when it comes to those who are different from us, is a normal part of our everyday lives. Our brain, if functioning correctly, is hardwired to experience, perpetuate, and act on bias. To have bias is to be human. During the Normalize phase, it can be incredibly helpful for leadership to develop and articulate a vision and specific goals for an equity effort. This goes back to our discussion of the "business reasons" for a focus on diversity, equity, or inclusion. This should be relatively easy because most organizations already have that pretty poster on the walls extolling their core values. There may be some questions though over why this particular equity issue should be the focus. This has been the case with many racial equity efforts for all the reasons we've talked about. While it is true that an equity lens is essential to bringing those values to life it may take some persistence to inculcate them into the minds and maybe even the hearts of your folks.

This is why normalizing bias tends to be the biggest stumbling block. For many, it is hard to accept the reality and the common presence of bias, whether the specific issues are racism, sexism, ageism, etc. In the beginning, you may notice that conversations around these biases will be difficult. People are often very sensitive and/or defensive when they talk about their own biases or the biases that are operating around them. Thus, the goal of this phase is to not only identify that bias exists but to begin to have conversations about what "we" as an organization can do to minimize its intrusion upon our productivity. It is important to push past the uncomfortableness and embrace the rich dialogue that is likely to manifest. During the Normalize phase, the ultimate objective is to make conversations around these issues a lot easier to have, not just in the presence of an external consultant but internally as well. I have observed that a useful starting point is making sure we all know what we mean when we talk about "D", "E", and "I" as well as bias, prejudice, stereotypes, and whatever other terms are important to the culture. It's a relatively easy conversation to have because no one is being put on the spot and if well-facilitated it can immediately generate productive discussion. This is another one of those ways we've made this harder. Half the time we're using words with no common understanding of what we intend to mean. I'm also *keen* on bringing up the "race is a social construct" concept. I find it amazing that we perpetuate such a concept that has no real foundation. "Race" suggests "inferiors" and "superiors." Ethnicity is all about cultural customs and manners. I've witnessed firsthand the change in people's thinking when they grasp this fact. I've also found it helpful to address the history of the issues as well. With such an incredible spread of generations in most workplaces, an understanding of how we got there is essential.

Often, it is easier to bring in us outside consultants to train staff and not necessarily involve the leadership team. Use outside support to open the conversation to reduce discomfort for employees who may not want to reveal themselves if the boss or supervisor is present and listening. Of course, it will be leadership's job, or their designee's, to implement any suggestions that are presented, but in this first phase, it can be more effective to bring in external help to get the conversation going. You knew I was going to say that, but it is true in the lion's share of situations.

During the Normalize phase, you should also make sure to present a wide definition of diversity although the equity effort is likely focused on a specific dimension. You are probably aware that in June of 2023 the Supreme Court held that Harvard College's admissions system did not comply with the principles of the equal protection clause embodied in Title VI of the Civil Rights Act. The Court ruled that race cannot be a factor in admissions decisions thereby forcing institutions of higher education to look for new ways to achieve diverse student bodies. Right away there was a cacophony of reactions. One that really amazed me was the pronouncement of the end of DEI! I mention this because it's indicative of the narrowness of how diversity is still viewed. (As an aside, I was really proud of my alma mater's response. Read it if you get the chance. In essence Harvard said that the opportunity for students to interact across a rich mosaic of cultures is a fundamental part of the education they receive.) It is important to normalize all aspects of diversity, not just the ones that people commonly associate with equity work. In doing so, the chances of creating broad support will increase dramatically.

Phase 2: Analyze and Prioritize

As the idea of bias is being normalized in your organization, the next step is to analyze and then prioritize the specific opportunities when it comes to addressing equity. In most cases this entails disaggregating the data to sharpen your strategy development. Disaggregating equity data is an essential step in understanding nuanced disparities within a population. To prioritize root causes and develop effective strategies, start by defining clear variables and categories, such as race, gender, and socioeconomic status. Collect comprehensive data using relevant sources and ensure intersectional analysis by considering how multiple factors intersect within each subgroup. Utilize statistical tools like cross-tabulations and descriptive analyses to reveal patterns and disparities among these subgroups. Visualize the data with charts or graphs to enhance accessibility.

Identifying root causes requires a deeper dive. Look beyond surface-level disparities and engage stakeholders, again including those directly affected by the inequities. Conduct a thorough review of existing policies and practices to determine their impact. Consider the historical context and systemic factors contributing to the observed inequities. Through this process, prioritize root causes based on severity, impact, and feasibility of intervention. Develop strategies that address these root causes directly, ensuring they are tailored to the unique needs of each subgroup. Periodically reassess and refine these strategies based on ongoing evaluation and feedback. Disaggregated data, coupled with a robust understanding of root causes, forms the foundation for targeted, impactful, and sustainable equity interventions. As we've discussed previously, this facility with data is the profound distinction between addressing equity versus diversity and inclusion.

Phase 3: Implement Solutions

Implementing strategies to rectify disparities identified in an equity initiative necessitates a multifaceted and proactive approach. Begin by translating data insights into targeted interventions, addressing root causes rather than surface-level symptoms. Develop inclusive policies and practices that accommodate the diverse needs of affected subgroups. Engage stakeholders, including those directly impacted, to ensure that the implemented strategies are culturally sensitive and resonate with the community. Establish clear performance metrics to measure the effectiveness of interventions and track progress over time. Regularly assess and refine strategies based on ongoing evaluations, adapting to evolving circumstances. Encourage transparency and accountability within the organization, fostering a culture that prioritizes equity. Leverage educational initiatives to raise awareness and promote understanding of the importance of equity. By fostering collaboration, embracing diverse perspectives, and continually reassessing and refining strategies, organizations can create lasting change and ultimately contribute to a more equitable and just society. If the stream of ideas around how to approach equity sound strangely like the basic mindset of a strategic planning effort, you're hearing clearly!

Concluding Comments

As a decision-maker, you can make choices that establish equity in your organization or social system. When it comes to racial equity, the context can be tricky. It is not always easy to talk about issues of bias and privilege when it comes to the color of your skin or other aspects of your identity. This section sought to provide helpful measures to promote equity in workplace systems and processes. We must first understand the problem if we are to fix it, and we must want to genuinely fix the problem if we are to succeed. The question is not so much "What can we do?" but "Are we willing to do it?"

CHAPTER 5

THE POWER OF INCLUSION

Here is yet another way we have made the DEI journey more arduous than it needs to be. I'm going to suggest that addressing inclusion before you tackle equity may be a better path forward. Yes, it's somewhat heretical given the issues of the day but my boots-on-the-ground experience with clients validates it. Indeed, there are exceptions. Public sector agencies that deliver services (recall Anita Friedman of Arlington County, Virginia) may need to prioritize equity. If you're a nonprofit delivering social services or an association like MEEA whose members are targeted at addressing disparities, it makes sense to go after equity. But I have seen too many racial equity efforts stall because the foundation was not properly laid. I feel like we have a brief window to make real progress and cannot afford the missteps that occurred in the 1990s. Frankly, there are still enough people that do not have a stake in the advancement of equity who would be just as happy if it went away. In many cases when we talk about addressing equity, in truth, it is a difficult concept to work with, and nearly impossible to get right, especially at the beginning of the journey. What is key to any transformational change is its sustainability, correct?

Equity is especially difficult to address in organizations that have dysfunctional cultures, strict hierarchies, and/or restrictive promotional practices. While measuring equity may be easy and changing it hard, the opposite can be said about inclusion. Data around inclusion is usually much more nuanced and usually takes more effort to collect; however, acting on that data can be a whole lot easier than trying to achieve pay equity across organizational members or equal representation at the leadership level. Those efforts will tend to take more time, and in some instances, a lot of time. Therefore, a concurrent focus on inclusion can make more sense if only to add momentum to equity.

When it comes to inclusion, there are multiple opportunities to address how much a person experiences a sense of belonging within a group, department, or organizational structure. When you focus on inclusion, you are trying to get a sense of what gets in the way of people bringing their full selves to work and contributing at the highest levels. Again, many organizations, when it comes to measuring the success of DEI initiatives, focus primarily on equity-related metrics. Unfortunately, these metrics can easily be skewed or manipulated and tell a different story. However, asking members in what ways their gender/race/sexual orientation/etc. gets in the way of their full and total participation generally provides a more accurate picture of how diversity dynamics are operating in the workplace.

You might find that organizational leaders are only giving lip service when it comes to DEI initiatives and do not truly support the changes they say they'd like to bring about. These leaders are inclined to direct the focus toward equity measures rather than inclusion measures, which makes the finish line harder to reach. When the organization is unsuccessful in reaching these high standards, the DEI initiative loses credibility and ultimately may not get taken much further.

An example of this was the use of affirmative action policies in the 1990's to combat racial discrimination in hiring practices. Many organizations gave opportunities intentionally to African Americans who were not prepared to be successful in the role. When they ultimately failed, an argument could be made that Blacks were not equipped to do the job. Another key example is the well-known "glass cliff" phenomenon that intentionally promotes women and other underrepresented populations to leadership positions under risky conditions, such as when a company has experienced a period of economic decline or during an organizational crisis. When these leaders fail, again it becomes a rallying point to justify their absence in the first place. Thus, focusing on inclusion first can be a more effective strategy than looking at equity measures alone. Good work in inclusion can support the sustainability that equity will require.

Achieving Inclusion

It is a myth that you need a different set of skills to deal with matters of inclusion than you need for just plain 'ole good management. A skilled manager, supervisor, or team leader is empathetic, trustworthy, communicates well, is trained in conflict resolution, and generally has all-around effective people skills. These are all the same competencies that are needed to attend to matters of cultural difference. When employees have high-quality management and supervision, they tend to have fewer issues in the long run when interacting with people from different backgrounds or personality types. Those who possess solid management, leadership, and supervisory skills are better able to detect problems before they blossom into larger affairs that can impact team cohesion, collaboration, and ultimately organizational functioning.

Take for example two employees who come from different ethnic backgrounds but also possess key differences in their Myers-Briggs personality types. When a conflict arises, a less competent manager may attribute the source of conflict to the fact that they come from different racioethnic backgrounds, whereas a skilled manager might realize that the difference comes from the fact that one individual is higher on "sensing" while the other is higher on "intuition", causing them to process decision making differently.

The employees in conflict need a manager who understands that employees can and do approach situations in different ways. Thus, a skilled manager knows how to intervene properly before the organization has a lawsuit on their hands. Too many issues get chalked up as illegal discrimination when the problem stems from an unrelated issue. Focusing on inclusion may be the best approach if you want to create long-term change and impact. That way the cases of actual illegal discrimination stand a better chance of being detected and confronted. I've seen this is my work with over forty federal agencies and departments. There tend to be lots and lots Equal Employment Opportunity (EEO)-related cases. This is based on the size, scope, and complexity of a public sector entity not necessarily its preponderance of bias. In 2020 the Equal Employment Opportunity Commission (EEOC) alone responded to over 470,000 calls to its toll-free number and more than 187,000 inquiries in field offices, including 122,775 inquiries through the online intake and appointment scheduling system. The agency resolved 70,804 charges in FY 2020 and increased its merit factor resolution rate to 17.4 percent from 15.6 percent the prior year. (Merit resolutions refers to charges that are resolved in the agency's administrative process (prelitigation) in favor of the individual who filed the charge.) Working closely with these organizations, you discover that a *lot* of these cases began with conflict that, had skilled supervision/management been present, an intervention could have occurred at the onset. Conflict avoidance is the enemy of inclusion. It also is the enemy of equity when there are too many cases to be given proper attention.

For most organizations, going from not even knowing what implicit bias is to solving equity problems may be too big of a leap. If we can't all agree that racism exists, then of course we can't address bias. However, if we address issues of inclusion first, we might be in a better position to achieve our objectives. Getting people to trust, cooperate, and share with one another is a far easier and more obtainable goal than achieving equity overnight. In this manner, inclusion is a helpful starting point and lever for sustainable change. Once you have achieved inclusion, you are in a better position to reengineer your processes and procedures and address any organizational bias that might be operating within them.

The final reason to consider a tandem focus on inclusion along with equity has to do with access to data. Given that equity will tend to center around areas like compensation, promotion, or performance evaluation, access to Human Resource and Personnel data is essential. The larger the organization the more likely it will be that these functions operate in a much more provincial fashion. In most cases, for a very good reason. Sharing HR data with DEI committees comprised of employees can be an issue. And when you are a larger entity there can be a lot of firewalls to data access as you can rightly imagine. When you start off with a focus on equity you better be sure that you have thought through these data access issues. If not, you will end up frustrating the equity effort as well as those committee members. Their passion for establishing equity is what led them to take on the task which, in nearly all instances, is an adjunct to their regular operational duties. That frustration will spread quickly. If you are not ready to provide data access, addressing inclusion can be invaluable in keeping that passion burning until you can get things organized. And face it, inclusion efforts can have just as significant an impact on organizational productivity and make work-life incredibly better for previously marginalized folks in the organization.

To be candid, I do fear that failure in making progress will cause the momentum behind DEI to be lost. If this window for equitable treatment of people in organizations closes now, what will it take to pry it open once again? I shudder at the thought.

Addressing Barriers to Individuals'/Teams' Full Participation

Again, while there is often ample quantitative data around measuring equity in an organization, the data around inclusion is much more elusive and generally anecdotal in nature. However, when you derive some central themes from surveys, focus groups, and interviews the anecdotes can be as reliable as any empirical data. This is especially true when you can collect specific examples of the issues that cause employees to lack the necessary sense of belonging. Central themes around inclusion typically stem from whether organizational members believe that a characteristic of their identity—be it their gender, race, sexual orientation, disability status, etc.—is getting in the way of their advancement. One barrier can be that in dysfunctional workplace cultures people are often inclined to keep quiet about the amount of bias they are experiencing due primarily to a lack of trust or confidence in the organizational system. That in itself is a huge data point!

As mentioned before, some barriers can stem from the leadership team or the executive functioning of the organization itself. Remember most organizations in the United States are headed by men who are not from an ethnic minority. As such, bringing up issues that concern underrepresented populations can be uncomfortable for many organizational leaders who may have limited firsthand experience with bias and illegal discrimination. As an organizational member from an underrepresented background, or as a change consultant invited to help facilitate DEI initiatives, you might encounter resistance at the very top when it comes to addressing DEI dynamics in the workplace. The harsh reality is that, at the extremes, this type of resistance can be a deal-killer. Over the course of my career, I have encountered a handful of client situations where this was the case and I had to decline the opportunity to work with them. As hard as it is to "leave money on the table" professional ethics and respect for the employees of those organizations outweighed the revenue. In any type of engagement, lack of sincerity in the C-suite ultimately leads to disappointment and frustration for employees who have invested themselves in bringing about positive change. In a DEI effort it is especially cruel.

This resistance should be expected and planned for accordingly. Nobody likes to hear that they have a problem in their own house. The very last thing you want to do is alienate the individuals who are in charge of enacting, creating, and sustaining change. Nor do you want leaders to believe that DEI efforts are a waste of time or company resources. The goal is not only to highlight areas of improvement but also to work toward meaningful solutions that empower everyone.

Addressing barriers to individuals' or teams' full participation is the first step in unlocking the power of inclusion. To do this of course, organizations should gather insights through a DEI audit or assessment. My approach is to conduct an all-hands survey that touches as many people as possible. This naturally includes employees but can also reach stakeholders and key customers, constituents, or donors. You will likely end up with a list of issues that need to be prioritized. It's not likely though hat you will be able to, or need to, address all of those issues. But you'll definitely want to put your energy into acting on the most egregious and productivity-limiting ones. I have a working hypothesis on what an organization's DEI issues are, but I test that hypothesis in each client situation to understand the level and degree of impact of each. Then I can drill down into the survey data, through any combination of analytics, focus groups and one-on-one interviews. These are incredibly useful because, in addition to getting targeted insights, practical solutions begin to emerge at the onset. It's paramount to get back to everyone who participated in the audit in some form. Not only are they not used to getting any feedback on organizational surveys, but reengaging them is a crucial momentum-builder! The very fact of knowing you were heard starts to chip away at the core concerns over inclusion, psychological safety, and lack of transparency. Plan your process carefully though. "Survey fatigue" can set in quickly and responsiveness and data quality will suffer.

These first steps contribute to establishing an environment that can support honest conversations about what is working and what's not. It is also important of course to act. One way that this can be achieved rapidly is through the use of implicit bias training for all organizational members including the leadership team. In doing so, members can better understand the factors that may or may not be at play during organizational decision-making. These trainings, often delivered by an external DEI expert, provide ample opportunities to have dialogue about differences. (Yes, I'm making a not-so-subtle pitch for us outside consultants!) Our expertise is in enabling participants to understand implicit bias as we talked about it earlier—as a normal dimension of being human and not being labeled as a "bad person." I have come to view this initial training and education as foundational to whatever may come next.

The unique aspect of implicit bias is that it can run counter to your conscious view of people and culture. In my trainings and facilitation sessions, I often share my own experience with implicit bias. I've had the great fortune of traveling to a good portion of the world, much of it as a consultant as well as through my love of exploring cultures. In several instances, I wasn't your garden variety tourist or vacationer. I had the opportunity to live with the people and really experience the culture. But you will find, as I did, that there is always a chance for those implicit biases to surface. I resided in Washington, DC, for a short time, in a diverse neighborhood on what is known as Capitol Hill. One day I was out and about and discovered that someone had opened a convenience store on the corner a few blocks from our townhouse. You need to know that I was born in Bluefield, West Virginia (yes, it is almost heaven). In Appalachia, the "corner store" is a significant landmark in many ways, so I was pumped to see one in my neighborhood. As I walked in, I noticed a man of Asian descent (I find out later that the family is Korean) behind the counter. He didn't appear very friendly, but I stretched out my hand and introduced myself. Not only did he not shake hands, but he backed away and looked at the ground. Determined, I noticed some small children playing on the floor near the back of the store. I walked in their direction, waving and making my best child-friendly funny faces, and immediately a woman came running from behind the counter yelling, "No, no, no, no, no, no!" I then said to myself, "Isn't this a blip? *These* people come into *my* neighborhood and can't even be civil."

A few years later, my wife was running for political office and got great financial and volunteer support from the Korean community. Whenever I was with her and they came around, I notice that my demeanor changed. I avoided conversations with them and couldn't wait to get away. Then it hit me! Despite a real, honest, egalitarian view of people and cultures, I didn't like Koreans. My brain recorded my experience with them as "unsafe," "negative," and "unfriendly" based on one unfortunate experience. Being in the field of DEI did not insulate from having an implicit bias. Thankfully, it did help me realize it and overcome it. Of course, I'm supposed to say that now some of my best friends are Korean. Well, yes, I do have some really good Korean friends, but it's not just because they're Korean. (I do love a good kimchi and a bowl of *tteokbokki.)* Here's an even more important point. It would have made a huge difference if I had known that some Asian cultures introduce themselves and show respect to a guest by bowing. Shaking hands is not necessarily part of their cultural customs. It would have been nice to have known that playing with their children without a proper family introduction isn't embraced. Even more so, if the Korean store owner had been given a few tips on how the folks in the neighborhood are likely to behave, he and his wife might have had a successful business and not have had to close up shop less than two years later. I'm guessing I wasn't the only one to experience a cultural collision.

It is important to remember that not all barriers to participation are real. You can't view every obstacle and challenge as an indicator of bias in the workplace. Not every obstacle is the result of your racioethnicity, your gender identity, your sexual orientation, or your disability status. It may very well be, but it is not always the case that you are experiencing bias and illegal discrimination because of these key social identity measures. It is important not to become overly sensitive when it comes to issues of difference, or you may find yourself out of the conversation unnecessarily.

Above all, whether as a consultant or as an organizational leader, it is important to help all members of the organization develop skills to learn and talk about bias that affects them and others. This is *essential* if you are ever going to get to achieve true inclusion, (and maybe ultimately equity), in an organizational system.

We'll talk more about some of the overall elements of an effective DEI effort, but interactive training and facilitation sessions of some type will generally be an important part of dealing with inclusion. In addition to implicit biases there are some other topics that should be considered. For example, it's helpful for us to know about microaggressions and microinequities, part of a larger field of DEI work in micromessaging. These are ways in which implicit bias might be inadvertently communicated in a workplace. Derald Wing Sue, a professor of counseling psychology at Columbia University, has a great definition of microaggression. Dr. Sue says that microaggressions are "the everyday slights, insults, putdowns, invalidations, and offensive behaviors that people experience in daily interactions with generally well-intentioned individuals who may be unaware that they have engaged in demeaning ways." I cannot tell you how many times a White person has said to me with an expression of extreme surprise, "Wow, LeRoy, you speak so well." I lost most of my West Virginia accent years ago except for Fri-dee (Friday) and hi-school (high school). But my mind (and brain) categorizes that comment as an indicator that they had different expectations of a Black person. You should check out the *I Too Am Harvard* video and article sponsored by the University's Office of Equity, Diversity, Inclusion, and Belonging. It's a real eye-opener about the reality of microaggressions and the unintended damage they can cause to a sense of inclusion and belonging. Microinequities are subtle actions that demean or marginalize someone. Always asking the female team members to get the donuts or take notes, constantly mispronouncing someone's name, not making eye contact, and confusing someone's ethnicity are all cited as common illustrations.

There is increased attention in the workplace as well to in-groups and out-groups. You will want to tread lightly in this area in my opinion. People have a natural tendency and a need for affinity and will gather (group) with others who share that affinity. In many cases, those groupings can be source of team unity and esprit de corps. Joining the staff book club, being on C shift, or participating in the football pool are all pretty benign in-groups. Sometimes, however, in-groups can be the by-product of bias, which almost automatically creates out-groups that in turn damage inclusion. Individuals with physical or cognitive challenges get left out of group invitations to try the new food truck at lunch or to hang out after work. Younger employees get left out of the informal project team meeting that happens after the formal meeting. The sales team feels like they are more important to the company than manufacturing. All subtle. All problematic. The best way to address the problems is to recognize them and begin to talk about them without criticism or finger-pointing.

Engagement of the Affected Groups

So what other approaches are being used to achieve greater inclusion? One of the best models is to engage the affected groups in decision-making and problem-solving. If you do not have enough diversity when it comes to gender or ethnicity, engage the members of the organization you do have, to better understand why, and what might be done to help.

You may have heard of Employee Resource Groups or ERGs. ERGs are incredibly effective ways of getting a pulse on what is going on with your underrepresented members. They also can give valuable input on a range of HR processes from the effectiveness of diversity training to staffing decisions. ERGs can also help you segue into new markets or cultural communities. Through leveraging relationships with like-minded individuals, ERGs can be an excellent way for senior leadership to engage with marginalized groups in their organization for example. Common affinity groups include African Americans, Asian Americans, LGBTQ+, people with disabilities, older workers, women, and working parents to name a few. Keep in mind once again that a "representation tax" can exist. This is the term for the stress that cultural minorities may feel when they are asked to engage in this work repeatedly.[39] Many DEI volunteers or board members are comprised of people who have experienced exclusion in the workplace (and sometimes inequity too). As such, members of marginalized groups may feel burned out when it comes to issues of belonging and inclusion. To mitigate this, organizational decision-makers should make sure to signal that DEI work is important to the business and work toward alleviating this tax (e.g., paid time off, access to mental health counselors, and compensation for DEI volunteers). Too often, we fail to engage the people who are treated unfairly. As a result, even more bias might be perpetuated in the system. In short, the people who are the focal point of your initiatives should be brought into the conversation.

---

[39] https://incafrica.com/joely-simon/how-to-keep-up-your-anti-racist-work-practices-6-months-after-george-floyds-death.html.

Managing "Tolerance"

It's important at this juncture say a quick word about the obvious. There will likely be those in the organization who will never get on board with all of this "inclusion stuff." There are myriad reasons for this. The most egregious is the reality of explicit bias. There are still people who *will not* accept the presence of those who are not like them, particularly as it concerns gender orientation, ethnicity, various types of ability, and age. Childhood trauma, deeply ingrained stereotypes, too may cultural collisions over their lifetime, and other incidences can rob one of the capacities for self-awareness and empathy. These all contribute to the hardening of the heart. And while that attitude towards others may be distasteful, people do have a right to their opinion. They do not, however, have a right to act on destructive and counterproductive opinions in the workplace. I have dealt with these individuals directly and personally. During my years of employment, almost of all the organizations I worked for had such folks, albeit in small numbers. In a few instances, the bias was explicit and chronic. Vitriolic enough that such treatment was the main catalyst for starting my own firm. (At least something good was born from the trauma.) I can easily say that my tenure with McKinsey was the notable exception. Were there people there who may have been strongly biased against me? Maybe. But I did not sense it, nor did I encounter it. To me, that type of culture is a great example of what we're talking about. At McKinsey the only barrier to inclusion was not being able to deliver high quality thought leadership in client engagements. And the firm's promotion and advancement systems supported that philosophy.

Across organizations, the fact that there can be illegal discrimination is only part of the picture. There are an awful lot of ways to convey dislike that cannot be quantified or easily qualified. It is therefore up to leadership, in the broadest sense, to establish a climate where those behaviors are not tolerated. The problem has been identifying what this looks like and where the point of demarcation is between the proper levels of tolerance that establish that climate. While not a precise science, I believe we can at least articulate the variables that we should be mindful of and describe what we likely see at each level.

	Approach to People	Attitude About Differences	Use of Negative Stereotypes	Willingness To Learn
I	Outgoing and Curious	Expresses Concerns	Breaks	Welcomes Opportunity
II	Curious but Careful	Couches Concerns	Unconsciously Reinforces	Sees Benefit of New Info
III	Detached	Complains "at home"	Selectively applies	Not Convinced of need to learn
IV	Privately Hostile	Covert Complainer	Consciously Reinforces	Resists Change that Knowledge Brings
V	Openly Hostile	Overt Complainer	Promotes	Denies need to learn

Figure 6. Levels of Tolerance

The key takeaway is that unless an organization can establish and maintain a Level 3 tolerance, it is going to be tough-sledding toward creating psychological safety. Lots of unproductive and dysfunctional interactions will probably still occur. But at least at Level 3, behaviors support core values and don't necessarily cause irreparable conflict. Because we are led to believe that the lion's share of bias is implicit, Level 3 also should sustain a critical mass of employees who can see the value of leveraging everyone's contribution.

Concluding Comments

The new frontier of diversity, equity, and inclusion work may well be about making sure that we fully address the opportunities of inclusion before we can expect to make sustainable progress toward equity. Again, inclusion is not the only goal, yet in some instances, it can be more readily accessible than achieving equity, especially at the onset of any DEI initiative. It is important to first open the door for honest conversations before we can aptly address larger issues of fairness and equal treatment across groups and in the way the work gets done. Remember, you can identify the problems, but it will be hard to sustain solutions if you do not foster a culture where you can have a sincere dialogue about what is going on beneath the surface of organizational life. Instead, make inclusion an equal priority and watch how it brings about better equity outcomes in the long run.

CHAPTER 6

KEYS TO SUCCESSFUL DEI INITIATIVES

So far, we have discussed why focusing on diversity, equity, and inclusion is an important goal for any organization. The question now is this: how do you bring about successful change? Let's begin to bring it all together.

1. Set Clear Objectives

- **Quantitative Goals:**
  - o **Employee Demographics:** Target a specific representation ratio for underrepresented groups within a defined period.
  - o **Promotion Metrics:** Track and aim for an increase in promotions for minority employees.
  - o **Pay Equality:** Monitor pay discrepancies and create a phased approach to achieving equal pay.
- **Qualitative Goals:**
  - o **Employee Feedback:** Utilize surveys and focus groups to gauge the sentiment and sense of belonging among employees.
  - o **Diverse Supplier Relationships:** Improve collaborations with suppliers and partners from diverse backgrounds.

In the context of a DEI initiative, setting clear goals creates the roadmap for evaluating success. It establishes a concrete path, offering both a starting point and a destination. These goals serve as practical benchmarks, ensuring that progress can be tracked and measured effectively. With clear objectives, you can align efforts, allocate resources efficiently, and monitor their commitment to diversity, equity, and inclusion. Without them, the initiative risks ambiguity and inefficiency, hindering meaningful change. In the business world, clarity of purpose is essential, and clear goals in DEI efforts are no exception, driving focused, measurable, and impactful outcomes.

Sometimes your DEI efforts can be directly related to how you measure your organization's effectiveness -the "bottom-line" so to speak. For example, if you are a nonprofit who serves the homeless and the effort you are putting forth is designed to help the homeless, you might have access to additional donors or the donors you do have may be more inclined to give more. It may be that implicit bias hurts customer service, which motivates them to go elsewhere, or that implicit bias impacts your outcomes with the populations that you serve. In any case, it is important for organizational members not to have a jaded view of DEI efforts, whether it's training on sexual harassment or implicit bias sessions. The best ways to accomplish this is by tying all efforts in this domain back to the core values of the organization and ultimately, the bottom line.

2. Assign Responsibility

- **DEI Committee:**
  - o **Composition:** Ensure a balanced representation from various departments, backgrounds, and seniority levels.
  - o **Mandate:** Define a clear mandate, such as making policy recommendations, reviewing progress, and/or organizing DEI events.

- **DEI Lead:**
  - o **Job Description:** Define clear responsibilities, including overseeing DEI programs, reporting progress, and driving cultural change.
  - o **Support Structure:** Ensure the DEI lead has sufficient resources, including a budget and team if necessary.
- **DEI Audit**
  - **Overcome Data Collection Challenges:**
    - ◇ **Data Availability and Accuracy:** Obtaining accurate and comprehensive data on various diversity dimensions, such as race, gender, ethnicity, and LGBTQ+ status, can be challenging. Incomplete or inaccurate data may hinder a thorough analysis of the current state of diversity within the organization.
    - ◇ **Complexity of Intersectionality**: Analyzing the intersectionality of different identity factors (e.g., race, gender, socioeconomic status) adds complexity to the audit. Understanding how these factors intersect and affect individuals' experiences requires a nuanced approach and may demand more sophisticated analysis tools.
    - ◇ **Limited Scope of Traditional Metrics**: Traditional metrics may not fully capture the intersectional experiences of individuals. For instance, focusing solely on gender or race may overlook the unique challenges faced by individuals at the intersection of multiple identities.
  - **Interview/Focus Groups:** Use these to drill down into the audit data.

Assigning responsibility is akin to designating a captain to steer the ship. It ensures that someone is accountable for navigating the sometimes-complex waters of diversity, equity, and inclusion. This responsible individual or team becomes the driving force, spearheading efforts, and making strategic decisions. They oversee the execution of action plans, track progress, and address challenges promptly. This step also fosters accountability and streamlines decision-making, preventing the initiative from floundering due to ambiguity or lack of direction. In any organizational initiative, accountability is paramount, and in DEI, it's no different – it's the compass guiding the journey toward an inclusive workplace or the correction of disparities. Here is what is really critical-be very, very, clear about what you want your DEI Committee to do and what are the boundaries of their role. For example, do they come up with ideas and then implement them or do they just make recommendations to senior leadership. All roles can be good ones, you just need to be clear on what they are.

Following the audit, focus groups are often used to get more context around the quantitative data. Focus groups are an important aspect of the data gathering process, as are individual interviews with key company stakeholders, which are both examples of qualitative data collection methods. Using the three in conjunction—surveys, focus groups, and interviews—can often highlight the bigger picture when it comes to the state of the organization. This audit then provides a helpful hypothesis about what is going on in the system.

After you conduct the audit, again remember to feed back the data to all of the people who were involved in the data collection. This step is crucial to build credibility and buy-in. The data feedback process is particularly important because you want to give people an understanding as to why the work is being conducted. Alerting people to what was found during the survey, focus groups, and interview process also furthers trust in the DEI initiative and ensures organizational members that their voices have been heard. Closing the feedback loop can also provide an opportunity to connect people to the business case for investing in improving DEI dynamics in the workplace.

3. Craft a DEI Action Plan

- **Short-Term Actions:**
  - o **Immediate Policies:** Introduce or revise policies that address pressing DEI issues.
  - o **Hiring Practices:** Introduce blind recruitment, diverse interview panels, and collaborate with minority-focused job platforms.
- **Long-Term Strategies:**
  - o **Mentorship Programs:** Establish programs to support underrepresented employees in their career growth.
  - o **Employee Resource Groups:** Support or create groups that cater to specific communities, e.g., Women in Tech, LGBTQ+ Allies, etc.

An action plan serves as the blueprint for progress. It transforms abstract intentions into concrete steps, outlining precisely what needs to be done and when. This plan assigns tasks, clarifies responsibilities, and allocates resources efficiently. It operates as a strategic guide, ensuring that the initiative remains on course and accountable. Without it, efforts can become disjointed and aimless. An action plan, in the realm of DEI, is like a well-structured project in business – it streamlines operations, sets priorities, and enables measurable progress, making the journey toward diversity, equity, and inclusion a purposeful and organized endeavor. Given the emotional context of many DEI issues, this streamlining helps to add useful objectivity.

4. Education and Training

- **DEI Training:**
  - o **Curriculum:** Ensure topics include unconscious bias, microaggressions, cultural sensitivity, and more. Use the audit data to direct your emphasis.

- o **External Facilitators:** Engage expert trainers who can bring valuable external perspectives.
- **Leadership Training:**
  - o **Inclusive Leadership:** Focus on empathy, active listening, and allyship.
  - o **Accountability:** Train leaders to be responsible for their team's DEI progress and culture.

High-quality education and training are essential to sustainable change. They equip employees with the knowledge and skills needed to navigate the complexities of diversity, equity, and inclusion. This education fosters awareness of biases, promotes cultural competence, and instills inclusive behaviors. Through training, teams learn to recognize and address illegal, as well as dysfunctional discriminatory practices, creating a more equitable work environment. Investing in education and training is akin to upgrading essential tools – it sharpens the workforce, enhancing their ability to make diversity work.

5. Policy Re-evaluation

- **Review Mechanism:**
  - o **DEI Lens:** Review company policies to identify biases, using an expert consultant if necessary.
  - o **Feedback Channels:** Allow employees to flag problematic policies or practices.
- **Recruitment & Promotion:**
  - o **Bias-Free Algorithms:** If using AI-driven tools for recruitment, ensure they are programmed without biases.
  - o **Promotion Criteria:** Ensure transparent criteria for promotions and growth.

The re-evaluation of policies and procedures is a strategic necessity. It ensures alignment with evolving standards of inclusivity and equity. As we've discussed, policies can inadvertently perpetuate biases or inequities, hindering progress. By scrutinizing and updating these guidelines, organizations demonstrate their commitment to creating a fair and diverse workplace. Re-evaluation also improves transparency, as clear and unbiased policies help to mitigate potential conflicts and legal risks. Policies and procedures act as the foundation upon which a company operates; reviewing and refining them in a DEI context is a fundamental step towards a more equitable and inclusive organizational culture.

6. Open Communication Channels

- **Feedback Mechanisms:**
  - o **Anonymity:** Allow employees to give anonymous feedback.
  - o **Open Door Policy:** Encourage leaders to be approachable for DEI discussions.
- **Regular Updates:**
  - o **Newsletter:** Dedicate a section to DEI updates in company newsletters.
  - o **Town Halls:** Have quarterly sessions focusing on DEI progress and discussions.

Open communication channels in a DEI initiative are the pragmatic linchpin for progress. They facilitate the exchange of ideas, feedback, and concerns, fostering an atmosphere of transparency and trust. By giving employees a platform to voice their perspectives and experiences, organizations gain invaluable insights to fine-tune strategies and address challenges effectively. These channels also serve as a conduit for disseminating information about DEI initiatives, keeping everyone informed and engaged. In the organizational context, open communication is akin to streamlined operations; it ensures the smooth flow of critical information, promoting a workplace culture where diversity, equity, and inclusion are not just goals, but everyday realities.

7. Recognize and Celebrate

- **Diverse Representation:**
  - o **Campaigns:** Highlight diverse employees in branding and promotional materials.
  - o **Success Stories:** Share success stories of employees from diverse backgrounds.
- **Cultural Events:**
  - o **Calendar Creation:** Develop a company-wide calendar of global cultural events.
  - o **Employee Involvement:** Encourage employees to introduce and lead celebrations from their own cultures.

Celebrating diversity and recognizing its contributions in a DEI initiative is another pragmatic investment. It helps engender that sense of belonging in a very basic way, motivating individuals to bring their unique perspectives and skills to the table. This inclusive atmosphere fosters innovation, enriches problem-solving, and enhances overall performance. Recognizing diversity's value demonstrates an organization's commitment to fairness and equity, reinforcing a positive workplace culture. Embracing diversity can't just be a feel-good gesture; it's a strategic advantage that can ultimately drive competitiveness and long-term success. It's a testament to the fact that diverse teams make better decisions and achieve more robust outcomes. This is something that we have always known and understood. In fact, as we enter into a post-COVID definition of what work looks like, these kinds of gatherings and celebrations take on a very different meaning. People value and desire social connection much, much more.

8. External Partnerships and Collaborations

- **DEI Networks:** Join networks or associations dedicated to DEI in the industry.
- **Supplier Diversity:**
  - o **Screening:** Use a DEI lens when selecting suppliers or vendors.
  - o **Collaborations:** Partner with businesses with culturally diverse ownership for various projects.

Engaging a broad spectrum of external parties in a DEI initiative enhances access to talent pools, suppliers, and partners, enriching the organization's perspective and resources. Collaborations with external DEI-focused organizations provide access to expertise and best practices, accelerating progress. Working with diverse suppliers not only aligns with DEI principles but can also yield cost efficiencies and foster innovation. These external relationships underscore a commitment to inclusivity and expand the organization's influence in promoting diversity and equity across the business ecosystem. Forging these types of partnerships is yet again a strategic imperative, reinforcing the value of diversity in all aspects of operation.

9. Embed DEI into the Company Culture

- **Integration:**
  - o **Onboarding:** Introduce DEI from day one for new employees.
  - o **Performance Metrics:** Make DEI a part of performance evaluation metrics for teams and managers.
- **Top Management:** Ensure that senior leaders are visible champions of DEI, setting the tone for the entire organization.

This is of course the most obvious but still compelling aspect. Embedding DEI into the organization should transform diversity, equity, and inclusion from mere buzzwords into integral components of the company culture. When DEI is woven into the fabric of daily operations, it influences decision-making, hiring practices, and interactions at all levels. This integration fosters an inclusive environment, attracting and retaining diverse talent, enhancing employee satisfaction, and ultimately driving business success. In the corporate world, organizations that embed DEI into their DNA not only reflect the values of a modern society but also gain a competitive edge, as they tap into a broader range of perspectives and expertise to fuel innovation and growth. To me, it's a lot like good strategic planning-you reach a place where you stop calling it "strategic planning"-it's just the way you operate.

I hope this detail is useful. DEI initiatives require the same discipline that you would employ for any strategic initiative.

In your long-term plan, it is imperative that you understand what you are looking for in terms of engagement, belonging, turnover, absenteeism, team cohesion, or whatever your priorities are as an organization. Again, measurement and evaluation are a key part of any DEI initiative.

Throughout your organizing efforts, you want to ensure that you maintain dialogue around the "tough" issues. In the education and training phase, the conversation got started, but it does not end there. You want to make sure that the conversation remains easy to have throughout. As you move forward, you will want to have more discussions about the application of DEI to the work that people do. This is a great topic for a brown bag lunch discussion or through a post-audit focus group. The intent of these discussions is less about learning what the problem is and more about determining the best way forward.

An underlying dimension of this approach is to focus on changing behavior first, not attitudes. Behaviors should be the starting point of any equity and inclusion initiative. It is very difficult to change feelings and ingrained thought processes. It is far easier to change behavior. Hopefully your efforts to change behavior will bring about attitude changes, but for the most part, attitudes should not be the focus or the target of your interventions. Instead, let people know how you expect them to act and watch how their behavior shifts accordingly. Surfacing implicit biases is one thing, but it means nothing if you don't instruct people on how to move going forward. Again, the core values that you have probably already established can serve as an anchor.

Throughout the implementation process, you also want to ensure that you commit to good management and leadership practices. It is hard to find supervisors who understand how to work with people just as it is can be hard to find leaders who understand that the role of employees is not to cater to upper management. Instead, the goal of leadership is to make everyone else's job easier. It is up to senior leadership to provide the container for equity and inclusion. If that is not the case, additional training at the top should be considered. Everyone in any kind of decision-making role should work toward building their capacities for leadership and, as such, better hone their skills when it comes to implementing and following through with DEI initiatives.

One way that you can train leaders is through executive coaching. Coaching can be conducted one-on-one or in a group setting, also known as team coaching. If you encounter recalcitrance or extremely uncooperative attitudes toward DEI efforts, coaching is one way to help unlock biased thinking and move toward more productive problem-solving. In this way, you can directly support any individual or group of individuals who are hesitant to get engaged in your effort.

Lastly, it is important to wean yourself from outside consultants and/or practitioners. Throughout the DEI initiative process, a good consultant should have built up your organization's internal capacity to handle diversity dynamics in your workplace. While consultants are great resources for the beginning and middle of DEI efforts, by the end, they should have worked themselves out of a job. In the long run, organizations should be able to sustain themselves and have all the tools they need to be successful moving forward. I'm guessing you didn't think I'd say that! But it's definitely true!

Most organizations do not tap their internal resources enough and can rely too heavily on outside help. When it comes to DEI work, organizations need to learn to be self-sufficient. While it can be helpful to have someone start the conversation, you will be far better off in the long run if those who are internal to the organization take up the mantle of change.

Concluding Comments

The processes and strategies discussed in this chapter are helpful guidelines for facilitating successful DEI efforts. We're also learning that it may be best to avoid "mandatory" participation in DEI activities at whatever cost. Of course, there may be a need for an initial normalization activity where you will want full participation. But the more you "mandate" the more you will create an atmosphere that produces increased resistance. Create compelling, engaging, and relevant experiences and the interest will spread. I regularly see this. People attending an initial implicit bias session that I am delivering are skeptical, feel put upon, and are hesitant to get involved. When the word gets out that "it was a lot better than I expected", subsequent sessions are alive with interaction. The goal of any DEI initiative is to give people a reason to buy in. Mandating participation over the long run can be counterproductive and move you further away from your equity and inclusion goals.

CHAPTER 7

DEI AND CHANGE MANAGEMENT

A change effort focused on diversity, equity, and inclusion is no different from any other change effort an organization undergoes. Indeed, all change efforts tend to embody the same stages and those impacted by the change exhibit similar emotional responses and behaviors. As a change leader, it is important to treat diversity, equity, and inclusion efforts with the same care and meticulousness that you would treat any other mission-critical transformation. But because it is inherently dealing with potentially emotional issues, it may demand a bit more oversight.

Remember that when it comes to achieving equity or inclusion metrics, the bar for progress can be daunting, especially if you are just beginning to recognize the opportunity. In many cases, trying to institute change around these metrics can bring on feelings of uncomfortableness that impede successful execution toward your goals. This is certainly true if the change is brought on as a reaction to illegally discriminatory practices, a response to negative events, or attempting to heal a dysfunctional organizational culture. Using tried and true change management models and strategies can help your effort progress. The key is to remain open-minded throughout the process and to celebrate the small wins that arise from each stage, especially the early ones.

Change and the Brain

In many ways, the emotions associated with the change process mimic the feelings that are brought up during the various stages of grief. One familiar model created by Swiss psychologist Dr. Elisabeth Kübler-Ross provides a helpful starting point when thinking about how a significant change can impact emotional responses in organizational systems. While the original model is based on the emotions and behaviors that emerge from dealing with death and dying, the lessons gleaned from this model can be applied to nearly every change management situation, including those that are focused on diversity, equity, and/or inclusion. It can be argued that people go through the same process when they are grieving that they go through when they experience a workplace change.

This process of change is not unlike other models of change management whereby the system goes through a period of shock, anger, acceptance, and finally commitment. Each stage of change serves a useful purpose that allows you to plan and implement the required change. A well-thought-out process can help eliminate some of the negative effects of change and get your key stakeholders on board faster, so it pays to be prepared. A summary of the four-phased process of change is illustrated below.

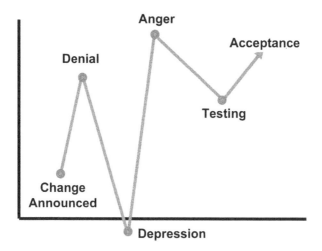

**Figure 7. Phases of Change Adapted
from the Kübler-Ross Model**

The first phase that is often felt when a change is initiated in an organization is *denial.* In this stage, denial is prevalent, especially in those who will feel the impact of the change the most. The denial phase happens soon after the change is announced. Experiencing denial is not a flawed human response. Your brain knows when it is facing something new and different and knows that a meltdown can happen if you take in too much change at once. Denial is the brain protecting itself from threat, and again, as mentioned in the second chapter, this is a normal part of brain functioning. When you are in denial, the brain blocks certain information to keep your neurobiology stable. If you are in a leadership position or in charge of instituting a change effort, it is important to apply this to your own emotional state and then to help your people get past this stage as soon as possible as it can be detrimental to progress to linger too long.

The second stage that you can expect people to experience is *anger,* which is understandable to a certain degree. Anger is a normal part of dealing with change and is another necessary part of the process. The appearance of anger, if it is not destructive, is an indicator that the change is starting to be processed by the brain. Holding in anger can be toxic though and can sometimes even result in somatic consequences. If anger is buried and not given an outlet, individual, team, and organizational productivity can suffer. As a change leader, it is your job to provide such outlets and to limit judgment on individuals who express vexation with the changes that the organization is undergoing. It then becomes the task of leadership to move folks out of this stage and on to the next one again as quickly as possible. Because diversity, equity, and inclusion issues can produce a visceral response, "letting go" can be challenging if not outright intimidating.

After the anger phase comes the *depression* phase, although this order can be reversed. Depression, like anger, can be a helpful part of the change management process. When change sinks in and you start to realize that you have to let go of the past, it can bring on depressive feelings. Depression is an indicator that the change is registering and can be expressed at the individual level, the team level, or throughout the organization. The best path forward is to progress through this stage quickly as possible, once again, without losing the value of it. It can be helpful to mourn the loss of a previous state, but like anger, it is best not to stay in this stage for too long. Change leaders should do what they can to help those who are stuck in this phase, but it is important not to rush any part of the process, including this instrumental step of healing, understanding, and internalization. In DEI initiatives, changes in organizational processes and systems can evoke fears of displacement, loss of position, and loss of power.

In the fourth stage, which is coined the *bargaining stage* in the Kübler-Ross model, your brain starts to process the change and understand that while things are not going to be the same as they once were, a future still exists. Bargaining is the brain's way of asking, "What part of what I am used to gets to come with me?" into that future. Understandably, people may have a lot of questions at this stage, especially regarding how the change will affect them personally. The task of the change leader in this phase is to continue to communicate what is going to happen and to answer all the questions that arise from various stakeholders. At this stage, the tone of the conversation begins to explore what stability in the system looks like. Again, as with all stages, leadership should provide ample opportunity for people to progress through this part of the process, for at the conclusion, change is finally established and accepted.

Understanding the Value of Repetition

With many change initiatives, especially when it comes to those involving diversity, equity, and inclusion, it is important to repeat your core messages as often as possible. One of the worst things we consultants have done to organizations is to keep introducing "new stuff" and often these new things are actually equal substitutes for the things you're already doing. Repetition is very important when it comes to change and should not be underestimated. Without repetition, our brain will not reach a place of safety easily. It is important to keep providing the same message(s) to people until they get it. The prefrontal cortex can only handle so much information. If information around the change is not repeated, it will not be stored in long-term memory. Many DEI efforts fail to get traction because the messaging from leadership is not repeated enough for the particulars of the effort to stick. To avoid this pitfall, repetition is necessary.

Repetition also helps to make the plan easier to follow. Research shows that repetition of information can convince people of its truth, which can be helpful when instituting a new policy or procedure. Stating the same thing repeatedly ensures that the message is more likely to stay in your mind as the more times a particular idea or concept is heard, the more likely it is to be remembered. Thus, as an organizational leader in charge of instituting change, especially around an emotional topic such as cultural dynamics in the workplace, it is important to repeat what needs to be understood whenever possible.

Lastly, repetition is essential when it comes to forming new habits and can help transition a skill from the conscious to the subconscious, making the task easier to perform over time. It is valuable to use all the existing communication channels available and perhaps even to develop some new ones. Given the emphasis on behavior this factor is critical.

The Long-Term Imperative

Clients speak of DEI as a "journey." They know that when you introduce a change that initially unsettles people, you want it to stand the test of time. Maintaining commitment to your goals, not just in the near future but for the long-term as well, is paramount if you truly want to embrace and honor your objectives. When it comes to diversity, equity, and inclusion efforts, make sure your timeline extends for months or even years into the future. It takes time for change to take hold, so as a changemaker, it is important to map out how this time should be spent and prepare yourself for the longer haul. This allows everyone to understand what will be expected from them now and down the road. The more you can convey to employees what the future is intended to look like the less instability their neurobiology will experience.

The reality is that here in the United States, equity, and even inclusion efforts are still relatively new initiatives. Today, racioethnic minorities are still subjected to unfair treatment in comparison to their counterparts, which is further evidence that it can take a long time for people to change their mindsets and behaviors. Take for example, the issue of racial equity relative to African Americans. For over four hundred years, individuals of African descent suffered at the hands of racial bigotry. Yet it is only in the last sixty years or so that that struggle has been a part of our mainstream awareness. It wasn't until after the Jim Crow era and the civil rights movement that it became acceptable to even talk publicly about racial inequality or inequity.

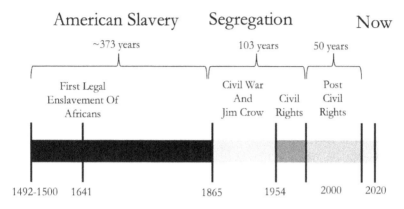

Figure 8. Racial Equity Timeline

While many African Americans and allies are understandably not happy with the slowness of the process of change, the reality is inescapable. Thus, if you are undergoing a change effort, specifically around DEI, it is important that you plan for the long run.

Plan for Resistance

As with any change effort, resistance is almost guaranteed. But it can be effectively managed if attention is paid to basic human needs. The fact that people have a problem with dealing with change should not be a surprise to those who understand the neurobiological response to the "new and different".

Resistance is a normal, natural, and unavoidable part of the change process because our brains seek to maintain homeostasis, or steady, stable conditions, to survive our environments. This state of balance is necessary for the body to function. As such, we as individuals constantly need to adjust to maintain equilibrium at multiple levels. As a change leader, planning for resistance can help you navigate difficult conversations and work toward more lasting change in your organization and its systems. When it comes to change, especially in the diversity, equity, and inclusion space, expect that organizational members may experience a disruption in technical, social, and personal equilibriums, and plan accordingly.

Technical Equilibrium

Technical equilibrium is disturbed when the change requires the development of a new skill or capacity. For many organizations seeking to implement diversity, equity, and inclusion initiatives, implicit bias is a relatively new concept for many people. Thus, it is not uncommon to have to change the way that you think about the workplace, develop new skills for self-awareness or empathy, and increase behavioral capacities for overall emotional intelligence. During the learning process, our brain has to rewire the way that it works, which is no small task and can be exhausting for staff and leadership alike. Therefore, when expecting people to learn new skills, plan for at least some level of resistance.

Social Equilibrium

Social equilibrium is disrupted when your social network or positioning is adjusted because of the change effort. Change can impact social equilibrium in many ways. For example, you may be used to working alone, but if your organization demands greater collaboration, this may result in a different way of gathering information, validating facts, and making decisions. Or because of COVID, you may have switched from an in-person working environment to a virtual environment, causing more stress for extroverts who value human interaction. And now for many organizations, switching back to coming into the office and other hybrid versions renews the disruption and possibly creating an even more intense level of resistance.

Whenever change impact levels of authority, who you get your information from, who you are in contact with, or where you fit in the "boxes and arrows" of the org chart, you can expect resistance. Even something as small as changing an office layout from private offices to shared offices can impact our social equilibrium. Thus, as a change leader, it is important to recognize when change will impact the social environment of your workforce and plan appropriately. This is naturally a core facet of DEI as the goal can be to increase the breadth of people who you to interact with. Add to that the potential for implicit or explicit biases to be present and social equilibrium may be drastically affected.

Personal Equilibrium

Lastly, during dedicated change efforts, one's personal equilibrium may also be disrupted, especially when it comes to instituting diversity-related initiatives. Personal equilibrium is connected to one's own preferences on how we do things, and it may be influenced by several factors from our personality to our circadian rhythms to even our culture. For example, some of us do our best work in the morning, whereas others work best in the evening. Others are more inclined towards teamwork whereas their counterparts may prefer to work alone. Some people may be very skeptical of the "new and different", whereas others are exhilarated by it. If the change impacts someone's personal equilibrium on an internal level, it can also lead to resistance toward your DEI effort. To combat this, strategies should be put in place to help minimize any potential negative effects brought on by change. And at the very least to provide safe outlets to express feelings and frustrations.

Overcommunicate

So clearly, change is not always an easy process to manage. However, there are tools and strategies that are available to help navigate even the toughest stages. The value of communication cannot be overlooked, and it is imperative throughout every stage of the change process. Stakeholders need to be kept in the loop and given information to understand why a change is being made and how it will affect them. By creating a plan and communicating it effectively, change leaders can help facilitate organizational transformation and will have a better chance of reaching their DEI goals.

As we've discussed, it is important to use all available channels. Newsletters, blogs, the intranet, staff meetings, team meetings, flyers, and email are just a few avenues that you can use to communicate what is going on with the change effort. If you don't overcommunicate, people will fill in the blanks with their own story to deal with the associated stress that comes from experiencing something "new and different". In most cases, the story that people tell themselves to explain what is happening is worse than what is actually occurring! During any change effort, and especially those regarding diversity, equity, and inclusion initiatives, this can be a dangerous situation. Consequently, it is important to ensure the accuracy of the narrative about the change effort by communicating, communicating often, and then communicating some more.

The Value of Transparency

Again, the narrative around change can be skewed if not enough information is given about why the change is occurring and what role each person plays in it. However, it is not just about giving information about the plan but also about being transparent about the process. Honest and transparent communication, in addition to increasing the likelihood of success for your organizational change effort, also inspires greater trust in leadership. Without trust, a diverse and inclusive workplace is not possible as systems without trust tend to have lower employee engagement, innovation, creativity, and ultimately productivity. Transparency is also important to hold the business accountable to their stated goals and objectives.

In today's organizational climate, transparency is also paramount as it leads to greater feelings of belonging, connection, and collaboration among and between colleagues. Transparency is not just talking about just the end result. Today, transparency also speaks to sharing the conversation that led to the conclusion or decision. Employees want to know not just the outcome but need as much information about how you got there. Stakeholders want to know about the various options that were considered, how those options were decided, and the associated risks with each alternative. The devil is in the details. Transparency throughout every stage of the process is one major way you can help influence and improve your change effort. Remember to share the conversation, not just the conclusion.

Reinforce the Impact on Organizational Productivity

Lastly, when managing change, it is important to keep your "eyes on the prize." Ultimately, efforts to increase equity and inclusion can improve or bolster organizational productivity. Making sure that people of all backgrounds and perspectives feel included, are represented in leadership, and feel empowered in their day-to-day activities, leads to better organizations that have better outcomes. Those outcomes impact customers, constituents, and donors. DEI efforts should be about making our organizations more effective and not simply a response to events operating in the external environment. It should not take the tragic passing of Trayvon Martin, George Floyd, Breanna Taylor, and Ahmaud Arbery for those in power to pay attention to the plight of ethnic minorities. Nor should it take the rise of the #MeToo movement and sexual harassment lawsuits for organizations to care about the impact of gender in the workplace. A company shouldn't have to lose market share to find out that manufacturing and sales don't understand each other and have reached the point where they don't want to either. A nonprofit shouldn't lose donors because its messaging did not appeal to the breadth of its current and prospective constituency. Instead, diversity, equity and inclusion initiatives should be initiated for a much simpler reason: it's good for business, whatever "business" you're in.

Better efforts when it comes to achieving equity and inclusion for diverse workplaces can ultimately lead to more efficiency and a happier workforce. Smart organizations remove barriers to full participation so that all employees can make their best contributions. In the end, attending to matters of diversity, equity, and inclusion is not just good for people who have historically been marginalized in the workplace but also for the bottom line.

EPILOGUE

I spend time, every now and then, imagining the future. I have two grandsons and think about what kind of world they will inherit. Will it be a place where you can almost predict the outcome of a person's life by one or two demographics? Will it be a place where hard work alone really does make the difference in your trajectory? When I watch television news, my perspective is often sobering. The problems we face in society seem insurmountable and there isn't much visible inertia to change that. When I look at my social media, I am a bit discouraged by what appears to be a wholesale lack of civility. Not uplifting at all. But then I spend time with the Anita Friedmans, the Tim Zilkes, and numerous others who work in the organizations I serve as clients and my spirit is lifted. I hear them having very courageous conversations, admitting that what they were taught as children may not have been accurate, and rekindling the expectation that their efforts to add value in the work they do can go forth unhindered. I have discovered that there is plenty of hope out there. There may well be many more "good" people who care about the plight of others than there are self-centered folks. There may well be many more leaders in organizations who get that trust is foundational than there are those who have a staggering inability to exhibit emotional intelligence. Yep, a lot of work needs to be done, but there is plenty of hope out there. If this book has encouraged you to look for the hope, then I have done my job.

Printed in the USA
CPSIA information can be obtained
at www.ICGtesting.com
JSHW020252140324
59111JS00002B/91

9 781665 754514